Praise for *Now Elected, Now What?*

"Chuck Namit has probably done as much or more research on school board governance than anyone else I know. Not only that, but he has taught it and lived it as a board trainer and as a school board director. All-in-all, Namit has developed a process that boards should consider if they are determined to improve achievement in their district. His work in this area will give them a solid foundation for improving the governance of the school district. Namit uses this book to describe various aspects of school governance and the latest thoughts regarding board decision-making, and adds his contribution: Values Governance®."
—**Nicholas D. Caruso**, senior staff associate for field service and coordi-
    nator of technology, Connecticut Association of Boards of Education

"Plenty has changed in America's classrooms. But is work in board rooms keeping pace? The hardest task for school boards is knowing where and how to focus their attention. Here are Namit's insights on how they can get a big-ger bang for their communities' buck."
—**Larry Swift**, former executive director, Washington
    State School Directors' Association (WSSDA)

"A 2001 Public Agenda survey of school administrators found that 69 percent of them felt that school board members micromanaged. Anecdotally, this continues to be a problem today and likely explains much of our nation's excessive superintendent turnover. *Now Elected, Now What?* describes the board's governance role in a manner that both new and veteran members will appreciate. This is a welcome resource to help board members better under-stand their role and value to our education system."
—**Steve Lamb**, former governance consultant/educator, California
    School Boards Association and Oregon School Boards Association

Now Elected, Now What?

Now Elected, Now What?

The Path to Successful School District Governance

Chuck Namit

ROWMAN & LITTLEFIELD
Lanham • Boulder • New York • London

Published by Rowman & Littlefield
A wholly owned subsidiary of The Rowman & Littlefield Publishing Group, Inc.
4501 Forbes Boulevard, Suite 200, Lanham, Maryland 20706
www.rowman.com

Unit A, Whitacre Mews, 26–34 Stannary Street, London SE11 4AB

British Library Cataloguing-in-Publication Information Available

Library of Congress Cataloging-in-Publication Data Available

ISBN 978-1-4758-3887-9 (cloth : alk. paper)
ISBN 978-1-4758-3888-6 (pbk. : alk. paper)

♾™ The paper used in this publication meets the minimum requirements of American National Standard for Information Sciences—Permanence of Paper for Printed Library Materials, ANSI/NISO Z39.48–1992.

Printed in the United States of America

Contents

Foreword

If you are a school board member or just thinking about becoming one, this book was written for you. Having been involved with schools and school boards for over forty years, I've witnessed firsthand the powerful effects a well-defined and well-implemented board governance model can have.

Not to be pejorative, but the vast majority of elected school board members share many common characteristics. They are honorable, well-meaning citizens who most likely have children in the local schools. They possess a volunteer spirit and are often members of one or more local service organizations, most certainly including their local school's parent teacher association (PTA). Then, because of pressure from friends and neighbors, and partly in their own family's interest, they decide to run for the local school board. This is all fine and good. It's clearly the American way.

But here's the rub—as a well-intended parent, the truth is you most likely have never been in charge of a multimillion dollar operation before, particularly one that is placed under the local and national microscope by folks ranging from the president of the United States on down to your local city council and news media. Schools are under enormous pressure to improve, and some of the finest minds in America are breaking their necks trying to figure out exactly how to do just that.

All of a sudden you've been elected—or you might be a board member with some experience—and you are a member of the board running the local school system—wow! As you might imagine, once seated, the job of school board member can quickly become overwhelming.

Newly minted school board members often bring no knowledge of *governance* to the job and only a limited understanding of *management*. Just like having attended school before, they also have worked for someone before.

Occasionally, but rarely, board members own or operate a small business, but that is infrequent, not because there aren't a lot of small businesses in America but more due to the onerous "public disclosure laws" in each state, requiring full disclosure of a business owner's customer base and all their creditors—something the real "pillars" in a community can't disclose without violating their customers' trust.

On the other hand, some board members have had formal classroom training in *management*, typically through a nearby college, business association, private vocational school, or even a local company.

The Boeing Company, for example, where I spent thirty-two years, had their own internal management-training program, a local library of books, plus video- and audiotaped lectures, and locally contracted seminars and study programs provided through the American Management Association (AMA). *Management* training was easy to come by but not *governance*. With all this, you can better understand why 99 percent of new board members come to their new position thinking they just got promoted to the top of the organization, that of boss-of-bosses, top of the management chain.

Even the national management expert and icon, Peter Drucker, had trouble going into depth on the role of the board, focusing instead on just the management equation. I've only been able to locate one rather short article concerning boardmanship titled "The Bored Board," (*Wharton Magazine*, Fall 1976).

In it Dr. Drucker identifies six essential functions of a board but never goes into enough detail so that one would know how to tackle the constantly overlapping relationship between the board and the chief executive officer (CEO). His six functions of an effective board were (1) assure competent top-level management, (2) make sure critical questions are being asked, (3) act as a conscience for the institution, (4) act as a "sounding board" or confidante to the CEO, (5) provide an outside "real-world" perspective to the CEO, and (6) act as an ambassador for the organization.

How can this book help? Chuck Namit understands the dilemma board members face. I first met Chuck in the mid-1980s when he was the director of School Board Development and Strategic Planning for the Washington State School Directors' Association (WSSDA). My job at the time was with the Boeing Company, headquartered in Seattle, Washington, where I was in charge of awarding grants to highly qualified education improvement programs. Chuck was one of those grant recipients.

As an elected school board member myself, I could clearly see the effects Chuck's training program was having on school boards. Later, in 2003, we both were drawn to a program that had taken hold in Colorado, referred to as Policy Governance®. After implementing the program with my local board in a Seattle suburb, I talked to Chuck about both of us attending the Dr. John Carver Policy Governance Academy in Atlanta, Georgia. That was the beginning of a major change in our thinking about boardmanship.

Attending the academy put Chuck on a path to delve even deeper into school board governance and the improvements it offered, most notably the difference between the board's role in *governing* and the superintendent's role in *managing* the organization.

When properly understood, the board's role becomes clear and doable. There's a very clear "aha" moment, which has become Chuck's driving force behind writing this book.

As you read through this book, you will see how Dr. John Carver has greatly influenced Chuck Namit's thinking, and rightly so. Prior to Dr. Carver's first book, *Boards That Make a Difference* (1990), there was very little understanding of the difference between governance and management. Today, Carver's conceptual model, referred to internationally as Policy Governance®, is arguably the most mentioned approach boards can name worldwide. Chuck might do well to have rephrased Sir Isaac Newton's famous quote, "If I see further, it is because I stand on the shoulders of giants." There are certainly other governance approaches today, but most of the creditable models, those that go down to the day-to-day role of the board, all began by using a base such as Policy Governance®.

With more boards implementing a formal governance model today, they have naturally begun to expand or modify how they operate to fit their own unique governance concerns. I would guess even John Carver expected some modification to occur over time.

In a private conversation at the end of the Carver Academy, Chuck and I spoke with John personally about the unique needs of publicly elected school boards and how the Carver model might need to become more specific toward dealing with the open public meeting act. He was quite understanding, saying he had been working at and designing his governance model for over forty years now and was sure it would evolve as more boards began to understand its value. He suggested that focusing on the unique needs of publicly elected school boards was a likely area for expansion.

With that in mind, this book, *Now Elected, Now What?* is available to help those who are driven to interrupt their personal lives and volunteer their time for the purpose of helping an organization they believe in. To me, there can be no finer group of people, nor no greater need than to make sure these people do not waste their time. They potentially have an important job and need to be allowed to ask important questions. For example, all organizations exist for a purpose. What could be simpler or more significant than to ask the following questions:

1. What difference the organization is to make?
2. For whom they are to make the difference?
3. Is the difference they are going to make worth what it will cost?

Only a governing board, separated from the day-to-day entanglement of customer relations, dealing with personnel issues, and making ends meet, can ask and answer questions like this. Unfortunately, without a strong governance model the tendency of most boards is to fall back toward a more familiar, super-manager role, wrapping themselves in what Chuck Namit calls the "valley of detail."

With proper guidance, it has been my experience that boards will see a good governance model as a stimulus—one that will move them toward higher levels of leadership, not just a way to reduce the normal board meeting drudgery, or as a way to simply "keep score" on the superintendent. If enough boards had moved toward a better governance model in our history, perhaps Peter Drucker might have been prompted to write a more upbeat article, one that could have been entitled "The Not-So-Bored Board."

Such is clearly the mission of this book.

— Bob Hughes

Bob Hughes is a retired Boeing executive and formerly an elected school board member with the Lake Washington School district (twenty-nine years) and the Washington State Board of Education (eight years). He has conducted numerous workshops and seminars for both the Washington State School Directors' Association (WSSDA) and the National School Boards Association (NSBA) and is a participant of the Carver Policy Governance Academy (2003). Mr. Hughes can be reached at bhughes@policygov.com.

Preface

The first insight for my book came from a Robert Redford movie, *The Candidate*. Redford plays Bill McKay, a handsome and nonpolitical person who has just won an election. At the end of the movie, McKay, the victor, speaks directly to the camera: "What do we do now?"

As a school board member, this is the question that many school board candidates have as they are elected or selected for office: Now what do I do?

You may answer: Well, I don't know!

Some school board members might then question themselves: Why did I run for the board? Maybe the board member can use the following to help figure out the answer:

1. I was asked by concerned citizens to run for the board.
2. I want to improve the school system for my kids.
3. I have to replace the principal.
4. I have to get rid of the superintendent.
5. I am a professional who can change the school.
6. I view a school board position as a stepping stone for future positions in politics.
7. I want to replace a school board member who dominates the board.

Many say these reasons listed are good reasons to run for the board! Or there may be another reason that hasn't been listed.

But the question remains: You've been elected. What do you do now?

Beyond your motivation for running for the office, you've got to find out some basic information on how to get the job done. Who has developed a guide to help answer this question? The answer: no one! That, of course, is the purpose of this book.

Although new board members can improve their skills from many of the lessons in this book, board members with some experience can objectively review their experiences and gain essential skills as well as more knowledge, information, and opportunities toward advanced boardmanship.

Acknowledgments

There are several people who helped me directly in the development of this book. My lovely wife—Patricia—has been very supportive of my career and the writing of this book. Several other people have also read, copyedited, and suggested changes and modifications: Rosemary Namit-Toth, Dr. David Steele, Larry Swift, Dr. Michael Boring, Sam Hunt, Aaron Owada, Joelle Steele, Barbara Fandrich, and Darla Buckley. The North Thurston Public Schools' staff have read and commented on the book: John Bash, former deputy superintendent; Raj Manhas, former superintendent; and Courtney Schrieve, director of communications/community relations. Tim Garchow, executive director of the Washington State School Directors' Association, has read and provided valuable assistance with other state and national school board associations.

There are several people and organizations that have supported me in my career in education: the colleges and universities that I attended, the federal government program "Teacher Corps," and the public school systems in which I taught and administered programs. I also appreciate the two education associations—Washington Association of School Administrators and the Washington State School Directors' Association—that gave me the opportunity to work and counsel closely with administrators and school board members. And finally, I truly appreciate the voters who elected me to a board member position on the North Thurston Public Schools.

Introduction

Typically, a person who runs for the school district board has many activities that will take up much time. Whether the board member has family responsibilities, work, or other activities, the time spent to learn some new skills and develop further knowledge is an additional responsibility.

DOES A BOARD MEMBER HAVE TO LEARN NEW SKILLS?

For years, many educators have counseled that it will take a board member at least a four-year term to get the hang of things. During the board member's first term, he or she will learn the traditions of a board. Many traditions of the board can be misguided. Unfortunately, a board member can learn ineffective habits and techniques. In a show of loyalty, the board member may well follow the traditions, so he or she doesn't violate the board's culture.

Consultants typically ask this question: How can we teach a board member the skills that he or she will need to do the best job? Starting with these new skills and progressing through applications and opportunities to grow these skills, this book is designed to help board members whether they are newly elected or have been a board member for a few years.

Learning the Structure of Governance and CEO Management in a School District

When you become a new board member—or you've been on the board for a while—you may have some questions about the structure of the school district. You may ask: What is good governance? And, most important, what elements or attributes constitute good governance and administration?

The Roles of Governance and Management

Here's a brief exploration of the roles of the leadership team comprised of the governance and administrative leaders:

1. The governance leaders: Board members are publically elected servants who serve on a school board for years. The board selects a chairperson or president of the board who speaks for the board in leadership activities. The board directs the school district by setting the direction through public policy and by selecting the leader of the organization, who is the superintendent or CEO.
2. The administrative leaders: The board selects a superintendent or CEO. The superintendent is responsible for the operational expectations of the school district that meet the board's direction. Typically, the superintendent hires a staff to carry out the required operations to meet the board's direction.

What Are the Elements of Governance and Management?

The elements of governance and management can be found in the work of the Institute on Governance—known as the IOG or the Institute—an international organization researching private- and public-sector governance, located in Ottawa, Canada.

These are the IOG-identified elements of governance and administration:

1. Work: These are the tasks that a board ("governance") and an administration ("management") need to perform as an organization to work together to meet the mission for the owners (the public).
2. Governance: This is the board's relationship with its owners and stakeholders to do the work of the organization and be accountable for its goals, results, or ends.
3. Management: This is the administrative component—CEO (superintendent) and administrators—that utilize the staff, relationships, and operating expectations to do the work of the organization.

These three elements—outlined in the IOG work by M. Gill Research—will be explored as we look over various governance systems while creating a new governance system that will assist school districts in their organizational governance. This new governance system is called Values Governance®.

ALL NONPROFIT ENTITIES AND PUBLIC SERVANTS CAN USE THIS BOOK

Although we have emphasized school board governance thus far in our discussion, many governance and leadership techniques and approaches that we discuss in this book are utilizable by other public-sector governance structures, such as city councils, county commissioners, and state and national public officials. Moreover, private nonprofit entities can use these governance tools.

THIS BOOK PRESENTS FOUR DIFFERENT STYLES OF GOVERNANCE

The most striking feature of school district governance is that there are currently three governance models in play: traditional governance; alternative governance models; Policy Governance® and Coherent Governance®; plus a new fourth governance model, Values Governance®.

The traditional governance model is used by most of the 14,000 school districts in the country, while 3 percent of the school districts use the alternative governance models. The two alternative models—Policy Governance® and Coherent Governance®—use universal principles of governance and four broad policy categories that define the roles of the board and the CEO.

As mentioned earlier, in this book we introduce the new governance system, Values Governance®, that adds new elements to help boards govern better. This system accepts the reality that most of the 14,000 school districts employ the traditional board governance but incorporates community process techniques and curricular and instructional innovations. This new model provides greater efficiency, effectiveness, and coherence in the governance of a board.

HOW TO USE THIS BOOK

Chapters 1–11 of this book can be called a "Survival Manual" as the information will provide newer board members with simple tools to become an effective member of the board, even in the first term. With the completion of this survival guide, the new board member is ready to join the board with some skills in hand.

The second part of the book (chapters 12–22) functions like a "Field Manual" with the purpose of increasing the skill and knowledge of board members, so they may gain additional skills through an *application* or further extend their knowledge by creating a new *opportunity* to learn. These chapters are titled Application-Opportunity A through J, for in-depth material.

So, whether you are a newly elected board member or have been a board member for a few years, there is information in this book that can help you.

Part 1

SURVIVAL MANUAL FOR
A BOARD MEMBER

People get excited when they bet on a card game. So let's use the metaphor of a card game to win chips and be successful as you read through the first eleven chapters of the survival guide that were promised in the Introduction. As you finish each chapter, you get one chip. When you finish the eleven chapters, you'll have enough chips to begin your board journey. You'll be able to play in the new Values Governance® game. As the board member motto reminds us: the difference between where we are (status quo) and where we want to be (your vision) is what we do. The survival guide will help you begin to understand your governance role.

DEVELOP A LEARNER'S ATTITUDE
ON THE FIRST DAY OF SERVICE

On the first day of your board service, adopt a learner's attitude: Acknowledge an acceptable level of detail about your school district—the goals, results, successes, and concerns, and so on; then, with your growing knowledge, commit to contributing to the district regularly.

A SURVIVAL GUIDE FOR A NEW BOARD
MEMBER IS NEEDED

As a survival trainer, I'll teach you some tools to help you survive in your new ordeal.

— William Toth, Lieutenant Colonel (Ret.) U.S. Air Force

Lt. Col. Toth, a military expert on survival training, knew that his new class of cadets would need survival skills, and in like manner school board members, too, need some survival tools to help them be successful. I am pleased to include such a survival guide in this book, and these tools address the following points:

1. What are the challenges that could face a board member?
2. How can we utilize the challenges?
3. Are there tools to help answer the challenges? What are they?
4. What are the resources that can be used?

Remember that the book is organized to also help you in your future board work. At the end of each chapter in part 1, "Survival Manual for a Board Member," chapters 1–11, we provide a reference to more advanced learning on the same topic in part 2, "Getting the Most Out of Your Board Service: A Field Manual for Board Members," chapters 12–22.

Mastering the eleven challenges of this survival guide assures you—whether you are a new board member or a board member with some experience—that with this training you will have the tools to do the job and be able to state: "When elected, here is how I will do my job."

Here is a brief preview of each of the challenges of the first eleven chapters, showing what you will face and then master in order to be most effective as a school board member.

Chapters 1–11: Eleven Challenges

1. Challenge: What is the work of the board and the CEO[1] in the traditional governance system? *We define the role of the board and the CEO in the traditional governance model.*
2. Challenge: What is the work of the board and the CEO in the alternative governance systems? *We define the role of the board and the CEO in the alternative governance models.*
3. Challenge: What is the work of the board in creating a new governance system? *We define the eight steps of Values Governance®.*
4. Challenge: As a board takes the initiative to develop its policies, it needs to know the principles of the board. *We establish principles for your governance.*
5. Challenge: How does a board member learn the work of the organization to accomplish goals and monitor the performance of the CEO for the owners? *We introduce the Mountain Peaks of Governance and Monitoring Organizational Expectations, as well as identify the parallel leadership of the chief governance officer (CGO) and the CEO.*

6. Challenge: How do we assess and evaluate the work of the board and the CEO? *We examine the assured accountability of board self-assessment and superintendent evaluation.*
7. Challenge: How can we judge the performance of schools? What can improve the learning of students in a school? *We review the ability to score schools on trust, relationship, and belief in schools.*
8. Challenge: Students and their education are the main purpose or product of a school district. Therefore, this question must be answered: What are the roles of the board and the CEO? *We recommend the adoption of a research-based or data-driven curriculum.*
9. Challenge: How can we gauge the depth of control that the board must have in directing the school district to meet the owners' expectations? *We establish a communication style and policy control status for the school district governance.*
10. Challenge: How do we engage in two-way listening and communication processes with the owners of our schools? *We introduce techniques to energize community engagement in two-way governance.*
11. Challenge: Is there a governance system that can improve the school district governance? *We introduce the new Values Governance® system model.*

Chapter 1

Traditional Governance System: Current Governance Method

Chapter challenge: What is the work of the board and the CEO in the traditional governance system?

In this chapter, we define the role of the board as the governors of the organization and the CEO as the manager of the organization. This method of governance is called the *traditional governance system*.[1]

GOVERNANCE SYSTEMS AROUND THE COUNTRY

"The U.S. has more than 14,000 public school districts and spends more than $500 billion on public elementary and secondary education each year (combined spending of federal, state, and local governments)."[2]

Most of the school boards across the country employ the traditional governance system. A small minority of the school boards uses other alternative systems—Policy Governance® and Coherent Governance® or other models—which are about 3 percent (an estimated 500) of the 14,000 school board governance systems. (Note: We will discuss the alternative governance systems in chapter 2.)

SETTING THE GOVERNANCE CLOCK TO THE FUTURE

The thesis behind this book is simple: we need to change the traditional governance model. The chief reasons for the change in the traditional board governance system are greater efficiency, effectiveness, and coherence in the governance structure and system. Since most of the 14,000 school districts employ traditional governance systems, any change in a board's governance system will require knowledge of other governance systems by the board and the administration.

DO BOARD MEMBERS MANAGE OR GOVERN
A SCHOOL DISTRICT?

The majority of elected school board members are honorable people who want to provide a service and give back to the community. These well-meaning citizens run for the board and are successful. But, as was mentioned in the foreword of this book, many board members view their board role as "managing the school district."

A conflict between a school board member and the superintendent is typical when a board member attempts to manage a school district. Conflict can be avoided by gaining a better understanding of the concepts of governance and management. Put simply, governance in a school district is the board's ability—through the use of policy—to set the direction for the school district. On the other hand, management comes into play when a board delegates to the superintendent the authority to use the operational expectations of the school district to meet the board's directed goals.

The most important element of governance systems is to identify the correct relationship between the board and the CEO.

Simply put: The board establishes the governance system and identifies the leaders' roles. Specifically, the board leads the governance system, while the CEO assists the board in the management of the governance system.

BASICS OF THE TRADITIONAL SCHOOL BOARD
GOVERNANCE MODEL

In the traditional governance system, many board members rely on the CEO (superintendent) to determine the relationship between the board and the CEO. The CEO identifies his or her relationship in the governance system and then identifies the board's role. We believe this is a completely faulty governance system, but it remains in place in many school districts.

GREEN-LINE CLOCK PROVIDES A TRAINING MODEL

In the 1980s, school board trainers were seeking a training model to differentiate the roles of the board member and the superintendent and demonstrate school district governance process. The National School Boards Association (NSBA) came up with a model of the Green-Line Clock that demonstrates the school board domain and the superintendent (administrative) domain. The NSBA model was called the Green-Line Clock (figure 1.1) that represented the traditional governance system for public schools.[3]

Specifically, the old-fashioned face of the clock on the Green-Line Clock was used to explain a school governance system. For example, NSBA asked the board members and the superintendent to imagine that a "green line" is painted on the clock that runs from 9:00 to 3:00.

Everything above the 9:00 and 3:00 is the board domain and is in the policy domain that the school board must deal with, while everything below the 9:00 and the 3:00 is in the administrative domain that falls under the control of the superintendent. The NSBA extended the model by having the board members and the superintendent identify items that belong to the board in the upper part of the clock, while superintendents did a similar task for the board members.

Green-Line Clock
The Traditional Governance Model
POLICY DOMAIN

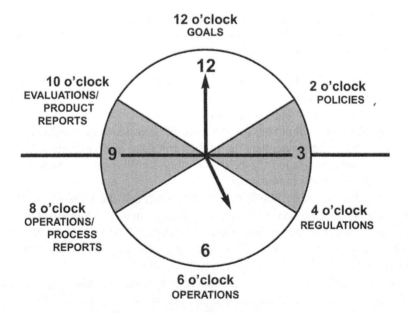

ADMINISTRATIVE DOMAIN

Figure 1.1.   Green-Line Clock: The Traditional Governance Model. *Source*: Copyright © 2002, David A. Steele, Professional Development Services

The points on the face of the clock represent the following:

12:00—Goals: The district-wide goals that address student outcomes.
2:00—Policies: General or global policy statements adopted by the school board to guide the professional staff in delivering the vision and goals set by the board at 12:00.
4:00—Regulations and procedures: Made by the professional staff, the means for achieving the 12:00 goals as established by the board.
6:00—Operations: Actual operations of the school district: teachers teaching, custodians cleaning, bus drivers driving, principals supervising, and so on.
8:00—Operations and process reports: Reports on the 6:00 operations indicate to the board and professional staff that the planned policies and regulations are accomplished.
10:00—Evaluations and product reports: Reports tell the board whether 12:00 goals are achieved. Periodically the board reviews its policies and modifies them as needed.

The triangular shaded area in the clock chart represents the difference in various school district governance cultures. As a long-term superintendent, David Steele, observed:

> Some school district boards go below the line, while some school administrators go above the line. Typically, the triangular area represents areas of tension that require careful attention.[4]

Simply put, it is what Peter Senge has called a "mental model." The board members and the superintendent can look at a clock and mentally fixate and identify their roles and responsibilities.

Although it is a simple design, it moved the board members and the superintendent toward an understanding of their roles and responsibilities. Specifically, consultants wanted the board members to eliminate the thought that they "manage" the school district.

In Washington state, the author further extended the Green-Line Clock model by telling the board members to "image" that their "wristwatch" was a board member's "governance clock." When the board members "think or talk" about governance and school district issues, they should look at their wristwatch and ask "Am I in my governance role?"

In the school district traditional governance model, we also added a *sideways pyramid*—that extended above and below the 9:00 and 3:00 hours—to designate that those *pyramid time periods* are an *interdiction zone*. The *interdiction zone* clearly indicates to the board members and the superintendent that they should not intrude into each other's domains.

The borderline—9:00 and 3:00 green line—is the *demarcation line* that allows each domain to determine its line of authority. In effect, it was a way to create boundaries for each domain to observe.

TRADITIONAL GOVERNANCE ELEMENTS

The traditional governance system emphasizes the need for clarity and coherence in the roles and responsibilities of the school board, the superintendent, and school administrators. Most governance models delineate the role of the school board as the governance team and chief executive officer (CEO or superintendent) as the leader of the management team. Together the governance team and the management team form the leadership team. The traditional governance system delineates the responsibilities of each role. Training in these responsibilities—which can also be a statutory requirement in many states—includes the following:

Policy development
Financial accountability
Board-superintendent relations
Community engagement and stakeholder linkages
Board self-assessment and superintendent evaluation

THE ATTRIBUTES OF THE ELEMENTS

The traditional governance system elements include the following:

1. Policy development: The school board performs its work through policy. Typically, state policy associations support school boards as they review board policies. In fact, the state school board association provides consultants who review a school with a district policy manual, and they recommend changes and work with the board to implement the changes. Integrated into the governance process are sample policies and training—provided by the state school board association and consultants—that provide the board and the CEO with a systematic approach to the development of school policies.
2. Curricular and instructional accountability: School district curriculum and instructional methods are vital parts of education achievement. Training in effective school research for the staff is also essential. Board members, too, can profit from manuals and training, which results in informed board decision making. On a federal and state level, the development of the

common core standards and smarter balanced assessments has a powerful effect on the school boards and the school district. The accountability system is transparent to the stakeholders and owners (the public).

3. Financial accountability: Boards are accountable to the owners for the financial health of school districts. Therefore, increasing the board's knowledge of school finance—through the delineation of the appropriate role of the board—is key to sound school governance and public confidence.

4. Board-superintendent relations: The centerpiece of a healthy school district is the relationship between the board and the superintendent. Training in boardmanship is a way to improve the relationship between the board and the superintendent. The training improves understanding of the roles and the responsibilities, and it creates clarity and purpose in the relationship.

5. Community engagement: Developing the board's awareness of the techniques and approaches of community engagement is vital to gaining community involvement and support of public education.

6. Board self-assessment and superintendent evaluation: An essential process for improving governance and skilled management is the utilization of board self-assessment and superintendent evaluation. The board can use these tools to provide accountability to stakeholders and owners for the governance and the management leadership of the school district. These techniques are essential to sound governance structure—no matter which governance model a board chooses.

WHAT WE'VE LEARNED IN THE CHAPTER

Chapter theme: Examining the traditional governance system.

1. The traditional governance system emphasizes the need for clarity and coherence in the roles and responsibilities of the school board and the superintendent.

2. The traditional governance system is the most popular. The National School Boards Association developed the Green-Line Clock model, using the face of a clock—the old-fashioned watch, not a digital model. The board must deal with the policy domain, with everything that runs above the 9:00 and the 3:00 hour. On the other hand, everything that runs below the 9:00 and the 3:00 hour is the administrative domain that falls under the control of the CEO or superintendent.

3. The traditional governance system developed the elements that delineate the responsibilities of each role, such as the following:

a. policy development
b. curricular and instructional accountability
c. financial accountability
d. board-superintendent relations
e. community engagement and stakeholder/owner linkages
f. board self-assessment and superintendent evaluation

THE NEXT CHAPTER

In chapter 2, we will examine alternative governance systems—John Carver's Policy Governance® system and Linda Dawson and Randy Quinn's Coherent Governance® system—detailing the similarity as well as the distinctions in each model.

More Advanced Information

As a new board member or a board member with some experience, you are not expected to read the more advanced information on the subject. However, at a later time, you can turn to chapter 12: Application-Opportunity A in the Field Manual.

Chapter 2

Alternative Governance Systems: Some New Methods in Governance

---

Chapter challenge: What is the work of the board and the CEO in the alternative governance system?

In this chapter, we will discuss the chapter challenge of defining and examining the role of the board and the CEO of the alternative governance systems—the Policy Governance® system and the Coherent Governance® system—and detail the similarities and distinctions in each model.

POLICY GOVERNANCE® IS PRINCIPLE DRIVEN

The starting point and foundation of John Carver's Policy Governance® model are based on a specific principle: "A governing board is accountable for the organization it governs . . . and it exists on behalf of a larger group of persons who, either legally or morally (nonprofit and public organizations do not have stockholders), own the organization."[1]

In practice, we can look at a set of principles (adapted from Carver's system) developed by the Missouri School Boards' Association that includes the following:

1. Trusteeship: The school board sits in trust for the ownership.
2. The board's job description is to (a) create a shared vision (ends), (b) connect with the owners (parents and patrons), (c) provide written explicit policies, and (d) assure school district performance.

3. The board develops a plan for accomplishing its own work. The board's job description is its perpetual agenda.
4. The school board prescribes the end(s) but stays out of the means except to say what is unacceptable.
5. The superintendent's job is to accomplish or move to the ends and not violate the limitations on means.
6. A board decision speaks with one voice [board].
7. Authority resides in the group board—not in individuals.[2]

FOUR POLICY CATEGORIES PROVIDE WRITTEN INSTRUCTION FOR THE BOARD AND CEO

John Carver said his Policy Governance® model is a revolution in boardroom behavior—since it is very "unlike the traditional governance model." Perhaps the most striking feature in both alternative governance models is that the governance model defines the role of the board and the CEO, and their responsibilities.[3]

Carver's Policy Governance® model is presented with four categories of board policies as per Carver:

1. Ends: The organizational "swap" with the world. What human needs are to be met, for whom, and at what cost or relative worth.
2. Executive limitation: Those principles of prudence and ethics that limit the choice of staff means (practices, activities, circumstances, methods).
3. Board-executive relationship: The manner in which power is passed to the executive machinery and assessment of the use of the power.
4. Board process: The manner in which the board represents the "ownership" and provides strategic leadership in the organization.[4]

The typical school district has a policy manual that is usually three inches thick. However, the Policy Governance® manual has "few policies—between thirty and forty—and is the focus of the board" and CEO's roles and responsibilities.[5] It is estimated that perhaps 500 school districts have adopted these alternative models to use as their governance model.

The school board's Policy Governance® processes and procedures include

1. reviewing "developing and modifying policies annually";
2. monitoring "ends and executive limitations policies through reports from the CEO or superintendent to the board";
3. assessing the board's work and evaluating the CEO/superintendent; and
4. holding linkage meetings with stakeholders to ask: "How are we doing?"
   A board can adopt another approach known as a "Carver Cop" to police

itself. This technique uses a board member to monitor the performance of the board and assesses whether the board stayed on task and did its "work during the board meeting."[6]

ANY REASONABLE INTERPRETATION

John Carver—in the Policy Governance® model—developed the concept he called "any reasonable interpretation" (ARI) that allows the CEO (or superintendent) those initiatives that he or she can make without board approval in pursuit of implementing a policy.[7]

In figure 2.1, we can see the comparison between *alternative governance systems*—Policy Governance® and Coherent Governance®. You'll notice that each of these models has four categories with similar names and deals with similar topics.

Coherent Governance® Is Similar to the Policy Governance® Model

Linda Dawson and Randy Quinn worked as consultants to assist clients in implementing the Policy Governance® model in school districts. The consultants, however, were aware of issues that face public education. For example, school boards must face the issues of instructional programs and

Policy Governance Model & Coherent Governance

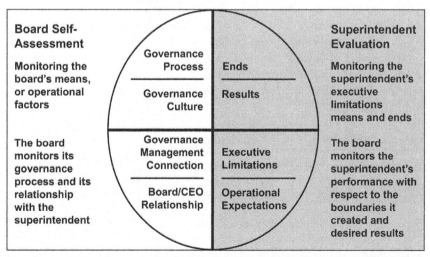

Figure 2.1. Policy Governance® and Coherent Governance®. *Source:* Copyright © 2016, Chuck Namit, Strategem LLC, Values Governance®

the quality of staff employed by the district, as well as other issues concerning such things as curriculum, assessment, accountability, and school district performance audits. Increasingly, state legislatures create new state requirements, and the federal government presses the state legislators to pass laws regarding specific policies to waive requirements. Publicly elected school board members regularly must discuss and develop policies that deal with means or operating expectations and issues. Simply put, school board members must obey the demands mandated by law. The Coherent Governance® system identifies the need to meet and obey the requirements of the state and federal statutes.

Dawson and Quinn developed the Coherent Governance® model—similar to other models—that comes "down on the side of encouraging the board to 'stake out its turf' in policy about any operational issue [on] which it has concern, to whatever level of concern it has, and then get out of operational decision making about those issues and delegate the rest to the CEO. Relegating the board to a bystander role in such areas of organizational decision making is not something we can defend . . . Coherent Governance® allows the board to reserve as much decision authority for itself as it must. . . . The caveat is that if the board makes the decisions, it, not the CEO, is accountable for the results. . . . Whenever the board stakes out its *degree of reserved authority*, from that point forward it delegates any additional related decision-making authority to its CEO."[8]

COMPARISON OF POLICY GOVERNANCE® AND COHERENT GOVERNANCE®

Authors Dawson and Quinn have developed an illustration that compares the Policy Governance® and Coherent Governance® model policy elements, which will show the similarities of each model.[9]

Note on the Policy Governance® and Coherent Governance® comparison model: Authors Dawson and Quinn have used the term "Governance Management Connection" for John Carver's policy term "Board-CEO Relationship" in table 2.1.

Table 2.1.   Policy Terms for Coherent Governance® and Policy Governance®

Policy Quadrant	Coherent Governance	Policy Governance
One	GC: Governance Culture	GP: Governance Process
Two	BCR: Board-CEO Relationship	GMC: Governance Management Connection
Three	OE: Operational Expectations	EL: Executive Limitations
Four	R: Results	E: Ends

Source: Linda J. Dawson and Randy Quinn, *Boards That Matter*, 2011, Preface X

In chapter 6, we will explore the importance of assessment of the board and the evaluation of the superintendent to improve the governance of the school district and improve the performance of the students.

CHANGING FROM THREE GOVERNANCE MODELS TO A NEW, MORE EFFICIENT GOVERNANCE SYSTEM

The most striking feature of school district governance is that there are currently three governance models in play: The traditional governance (discussed in chapter 1) and two alternative governance models—Policy Governance® and Coherent Governance® (discussed in this chapter).

The traditional governance model is used by most of the 14,000 school districts in the country, while 3 percent of the school districts use an alternative governance model. The alternative models—the Policy Governance® and Coherent Governance® systems—use universal principles of governance and four broad policy categories that define the role of the board and the CEO.

In this book, we want to create a *new governance system* that will add new elements to help boards to govern better. We will introduce a fourth model called the Values Governance® system that accepts the reality that most of the 14,000 school districts employ the traditional board governance but incorporates community process techniques and curricular and instructional innovations. This new model provides greater efficiency, effectiveness, and coherence in the governance of a board.

WHAT WE'VE LEARNED IN THE CHAPTER

Chapter theme: Examining the alternative governance models.

1. There are 14,000 public school districts across the nation. Most of these public school systems follow a traditional governance model of education. Alternative governance models have been introduced to modify the governance process since the mid-1990s.
2. In 1990, John Carver introduced the Policy Governance® model, and Linda J. Dawson and Randy Quinn introduced the Coherent Governance® model in 2011. Of the 14,000 school districts around the country, approximately 500 school districts use the alternative systems of governance.
3. If a board adopts either of the alternative governance models, Policy Governance® or Coherent Governance®, there must be changes in the structure of governance. These changes include adoption of the quadrant model of board policies that features: Governance Process (governance culture),

Governance Management Connection (board-CEO relationship), Executive Limitation (operational expectations), and Ends (results) policies.
4. Adopt a new governance system that incorporates community process techniques, as well as curricular and instructional innovations.

THE NEXT SECTION: TURNING TO A NEW GOVERNANCE MODEL

In the next section of this book, chapters 3 through 11, we will introduce a new enhanced school district governance model that we call Values Governance®. The new model enhances the traditional governance system that is used by most public schools around the country.

More Advanced Information

As a new board member or a board member with some experience, you are not expected to read the more advanced information on the subject. However, at a later time, you can turn to chapter 13: Application-Opportunity B in the Field Manual.

Chapter 3

Turning to a New Governance Model: Values Governance® System

Chapter challenge: What is the work of the board in creating a new governance system?

In chapters 1 and 2, we outlined the three major governing systems for the public schools—traditional governance, Policy Governance®, and Coherence Governance®. Traditional governance systems account for almost 14,000 districts while several hundred systems have chosen to enact either Policy Governance® or Coherence Governance®.

Larry Swift—former executive director of the Washington State School Directors' Association and the original Shannon Award winner of the National School Boards Association—made this astute observation:

"Showing the evolution of the theoretical foundation of school board work is important for new board members. Their central challenge is to develop a working understanding of the difference between governance and management. And, of course, addressing that distinction is at the heart of the traditional governance model, Carver's Policy Governance®, Quinn and Dawson's Coherent Governance®, and the author's Values Governance®. . . . After they get their feet on the ground, new board members need to see how to put those theoretical ideas to work in the real world of school boarding.

Too often when told to keep their actions above the 'green governance line,' new board members feel that they can't have any significant impact on district affairs, because the 'real' power is in management. . . . Clarifying the differences between the several governance models shows the *evolutionary progress* that has occurred in thinking about governance. Such an overview should help new board members see the importance of spending time think-ing about the *philosophical underpinnings* of their new role."

"CALL IN THE CHIPS" FOR ALL GOVERNANCE MODELS

Card games have a saying to "call in the chips." So let's call in the chips for all the governance models that we've discussed so far in the book to see what each model has provided new board members in an evolutionary sense. Here's a roll call with a brief highlight of the models for board member assessment:

- Traditional Governance model: The NSBA offered a real transition in the development of school governance by a Green-Line Clock model that pro-vides a division of authority that designated a board domain and manage-ment domain of authority. In a very real sense, this allows the board and CEO to identify each other's roles and responsibilities.
- Policy Governance® model: John Carver then developed a model based on the board members and the community's beliefs and values. His gov-ernance model created four distinct board policy categories that further defined the board's authority to set the direction for the school district. He also added the essential concept of in-depth monitoring of the board and superintendent actions.
- Coherent Governance® model: Randy Quinn and Linda Dawson created a governance model that is similar to the Policy Governance® model, with the sharp distinction that the board can stake out turf or create a degree of reserved authority in the area of curriculum and instruction.

TURNING TO A NEW MODEL

The next model that we discuss throughout the rest of the book is called the Values Governance® model. This governance model incorporates the features of the three previous governance models, with the added innovation of the Sky Bridge of Monitoring to assure compliance with the board's direction setting. It also incorporates—for board members—their input into the cur-riculum and instructional issues before turning that process over to the CEO for implementation.

This new, potent enhancement to governance systems, the Values Gov-ernance® system, explicitly enhances the traditional governance system and provides insight, tools, and achievable results.

WHY DO WE CALL IT VALUES GOVERNANCE®?

The dictionary defines values as "a principle or standard, as of behavior that is considered important or desirable." In terms of board behavior, values guide the actions of its members as they lead the organization to improve the education of children.

The first step of our Values Governance® system begins with the identification of school board members' universal values and principles to help identify the board's direction. Indeed, these values form the foundation of its governance system. Therefore, each of the areas listed in chapters 3 through 11—when taken together—guide a board to be more successful.

Begin Your Values Governance® Experience

The rest of this book introduces the eight steps of the Values Governance® system that change and enhance the traditional governance system.

The Values Governance® system modifies some governance elements of the three governance models. It adds new governance elements—new concepts, tools, and practices—that give board members an enhanced view of their new governance system. Here's a brief summary of the Values Governance® system in the steps numbered 1–8 presented in the rest of the book from chapters 4 through 11:

Step 1: In chapter 4, the board identifies its beliefs and principles, in order to develop its governing system.

Step 2: In chapter 5, we present the Mountain Peaks of Governance and Monitoring Organizational Expectations—these provide more efficiency and consistency in governing the school district.

Step 3: In chapter 6, the annual board self-assessment and superintendent evaluation processes provide a measure of assurance to the community regarding the governance of the public schools.

Step 4: In chapter 7, the four phases of school-community engagement process allow the board to gauge the community support for its public schools.

Step 5: In chapter 8, the school district develops a research-based curriculum that increases student learning and improves the public schools.

Step 6: In chapter 9, board members learn their communication style and the policy control status for governing the organization.

Step 7: In chapter 10, the board *energizes community engagement in a two-way governance* approach that engages the community in the work of the school district.

Step 8: In chapter 11, we engage the board members in a student learning discussion while pulling together all the elements of the Values Governance® system.

WHAT WE'VE LEARNED IN THE CHAPTER

Chapter theme: Turning to a new governance model.

1. The theoretical foundation of the school board is to determine the difference between management and governance to achieve increased student achievement.
2. We discussed the traditional governance and the alternative governance systems—Policy Governance® and Coherent Governance® systems.
3. We presented the advantages of Values Governance® as well as summarized the eight steps to achieving the Values Governance® system.

THE NEXT CHAPTER

In chapter 4, we will discuss the board and CEO (superintendent) relationship and leadership. The board develops accepted beliefs and universal beliefs that form the basis of the school district governance ship of state.

More Advanced Information

As a new board member or a board member with some experience, you will be introduced to a new governance system called Values Governance®. You can turn to chapter 14: Application-Opportunity in the Field Manual.

Chapter 4

Establishing Principles for Your Governance

Chapter challenge: As a board takes the initiative to develop its policies, it needs to know the principles of the board.

Step 1: Values Governance® System

This chapter offers the board the opportunity to review and understand the community beliefs and principles that will define and strengthen their governance for the school district.

Board Discusses Community Beliefs and Principles

The school board can learn from the John Carver and Dawson/Quinn models by taking its first step: the school board should be engaged in a process to examine the school district values. The development of the school district values will form the basis of developing a set of policies for a locally developed governance model.

Although school boards have a similar structure (responsibilities and roles) and carry out similar functions and practices, they do not all look alike. The differences in school districts are due, in large part, to the differences in the constituencies they serve and the common experiences that board members may share based on school board history and community values.

Though a board may have a school board history, it can develop its own governance model based on values that affect the community by answering these questions:

1. What constitutes governance?
2. What does an effective governance system look like in our school district?

Board members can do some research to determine what constitutes a good governance model. Some of the books that provide a traditional governance and alternative governance models include the following: National School Boards Association, *Becoming a Better Board Member: A Guide to Effective School Board Service;* John Carver and Miriam Mayhew Carver, *Reinventing your Board;* and Linda J. Dawson and Randy Quinn, *Good Governance Is a Choice and Boards That Matter.*

KEY AREA 1—DEVELOPING YOUR UNIVERSAL PRINCIPLE LIST

Universal principles or statements indicate what the board wants to do or where the board wants to go in developing its goals, ends, or results for the organization. In effect, universal principles are "direction setting." *Nonuniversal principles* indicate how and who in the organization—CEO or delegated staff—will do it. These nonuniversal principles are the super-intendent's function and describe what he or she will do to accomplish the task. The board employs the superintendent to specify how it will be done to accomplish or reach the goals or results that the board prescribes.

Rule of thumb: A universal principle is one that provides a direction to the board in establishing or setting an activity, whereas the nonuniversal principle directs the CEO toward an activity that has operational expectations. Since we are establishing a board governance system, we want only universal principles in developing our new governance model.

Exercise in Developing a Universal Principle List

One of the roles of a consultant is typically to assist a client school district in developing its universal principles of governance. This is an exercise that John Carver used in training a policy governance consultant class with a goal of developing a set of universal principles.

During the five-day intensive training at the Policy Governance Academy by John and Miriam Carver—October 20–24, 2003—students were given an exercise to begin a class on Policy Governance®. All the statements listed later are from an academy class that developed a list of universal principles. The class then discussed each statement to determine whether it had a universal quality that made it eligible for the list of principles to govern. However, certain statements were judged as nonuniversal statements and stricken from the list. (Note: The numbers 6, 7, and 15 were considered nonuniversal statements by the consultants; therefore, we will examine each of these statements—6, 7, and 15—and provide a brief comment. These three statements are typed in **boldface**.)

This is the list developed by the Policy Governance® class:

1. The board governs through written policies.
2. Proscriptive statements (written in the negative) are means (operating expectations or executive limitations) statements that are written by the board for the CEO.
3. The board speaks with one voice or not at all.
4. Policies have distinct role definitions (e.g., board, CEO, owner).
5. The board determines policies for the quadrant (governance process, board-CEO relations, executive limitations, and ends).
6. **Diverse opinions are encouraged. (This is a statement that *does not* provide a direction-setting perspective for a board.)**
7. **Boards control the strategic planning process. (This is the CEO's responsibility since it deals with operational expectations.)**
8. The board monitors the CEO's performance in the organization.
9. Anything that is not an ends (goals or results) statement is a means (operating expectations) statement.
10. Board's policies must be very carefully crafted.
11. The board is responsible for its own agenda.
12. The board members must listen to the community (linkage meetings).
13. The board must do a summative evaluation of the CEO.
14. The board delegates tasks to the CEO.
15. **The board and the superintendent share in the decision making. (This statement does not distinguish between the board and the superintendent roles; specifically, the board sets the direction for the district through policy and then delegates responsibilities to the CEO to fulfill the direction-setting policy, goal, etc., through operational expectations.)**

As you go through this exercise to develop your own universal statements, you can examine your list with the policy governance class list to compare and interpret which of your statements are universal principles.

This exercise is absolutely essential for the foundation of your governance process. Now, it is your turn to use this exercise to develop your own universal principles for your governance model.

KEY AREA 2—A BOARD EXERCISE: DEVELOPING UNIVERSAL GOVERNANCE PRINCIPLES

Board members need to define their communication styles, management, and governance styles and discuss their principle in the school district governance. The next step is to look at the board's principles that give board

Table 4.1.   Universal Principles for Governance List

List of Principles	Universal	Nonuniversal
1.		
2.		
3.		
4.		
5.		
6.		
7.		
8.		
9.		
10.		
11.		
12.		

Source: Copyright © 2016, Chuck Namit, Strategem LLC, Values Governance®

members another piece of the puzzle: a viable board must have a sense of the school district leadership direction. Now, school board members can use the exercise to develop their own universal principles for school governance.

Consultants—during John Carver's Advanced Policy Governance Academy in 2003—used an exercise with a Policy Governance® model to develop some universal principles that apply to governance model. School board members can use this same exercise to design the school district governance model. Here are the steps that the board can use:

1. Board members should list universal principles for their school district.
2. Once the list is developed, then the group reviews the list and narrows down to the agreed upon universal principles.
3. Once the list of universal principles is developed and agreed upon, then the group begins to discuss ways that the list can be used to develop a governance model to improve the school district.

Develop a List of Universal Principles for Governance

Directions: The board should develop a list of universal principles—the board to direct the organization and the CEO to use as operational expectations—and list them on the form (see table 4.1, "Universal Principles for Governance List"). The board will review the list and check whether they are *universal* or *nonuniversal* principles.

Forming the "Keel" of Your Governance Ship of State

Imagine the board, administration, and the community is forming the school district's Governance Ship of State. Two steps are taken:

1. Review the universal principles that the board members and the school administrators develop. How do they represent your school district's owners (parents, students, teachers, administrators, businesses, community, etc.)?
2. Engage the owners in the discussion of the new governance system. The goal of the discussion is to develop a governance system that improves the learning of students while improving the school district.

WHAT WE'VE LEARNED IN THE CHAPTER

Chapter theme: The board develops a list of beliefs and principles to define their future governance model.

1. Discuss the differences between universal and nonuniversal principles.
2. The board then develops a list of beliefs and universal principles.

3. Use the accepted beliefs and universal principles to form the "keel" of the school district governance ship of state.

THE NEXT CHAPTER

In chapter 5, we will introduce Mountain Peaks of Governance and Monitoring Organizational Expectations, as well as the parallel-leadership structure of a school district.

More Advanced Information

As a new board member or a board member with some experience, you will be introduced to a new governance system called Values Governance®. You can turn to chapter 14: Application-Opportunity in the Field Manual.

Chapter 5

Mountain Peaks of Governance: Developing the Sky Bridge of Monitoring

Chapter challenge: How does a board member learn the work of the organization to accomplish goals, and monitor the performance of the CEO for the owners? Values Governance® System

Step 2: Values Governance® System

In chapter 3, we discussed the importance of the board developing universal values as the basis for developing the school district governance principles. The board—as an ongoing process—needs to periodically examine its own and community values, beliefs, and principles. The board provides guidance and direction in setting forth the organization to meet the owners' needs.

In this chapter, we will introduce Mountain Peaks of Governance and Monitoring Organizational Expectations, as well as identify the parallel leadership of the chief governance officer (CGO) or school board president and the CEO or superintendent who leads the management of the organization. We will discuss the critical Mountain Peaks of Governance and the vital relationship of the board and CEO relationship and leadership.

The role of the parallel leadership demonstrates the board's leadership role in policies and important decisions, while figuratively sending the CEO down off the mountaintop and into the "valley of detail" to work through the operational expectations (means) of dealing with governance. Simply put, there is not a better way to explain the roles of the board and the CEO. The goal is to have board members understand their role and the role of the CEO or superintendent.

As we mentioned in our introduction to the Values Governance® system, we will take some elements of the three governance models—new concepts, tools, and practices—and add new elements. And so it is with this chapter.

MOUNTAIN PEAKS OF GOVERNANCE
AND LEADERSHIP DEVELOPMENT

A pastor gave a sermon on the theory of prophecy that can apply to a governance model. The early prophets would climb a mountain peak to get closer to a higher being. Once the prophets reached the mountaintop and viewed the distant peaks, they would look out into the future and see a vision or prophecy.

The board can use this model to present a vision of the future for the school district. The board may well ask these questions:

1. How could a board go from the ascended peak to a distant peak to gain the fulfillment of the vision (goal, result, or end)?
2. Will the board have to descend from the mountain peak—going down into the valley of detail—where administrators do their operational work?
3. How can the board stay out of the CEO's "valley of detail"?

This last question is a vital one for board members. When you answer these questions, a Mountain Peak of Governance arises.

Using the Mountain Peaks Analogy for Inspiration

Even though the board—accompanied by the superintendent—climbs the peak to develop a new policy on the initial peak of inspiration, the board is faced with a problem.

Figure 5.1 shows the Mountain Peaks of Governance model. The board needs a "sky bridge" to stretch across to the distant peak—and accomplish the

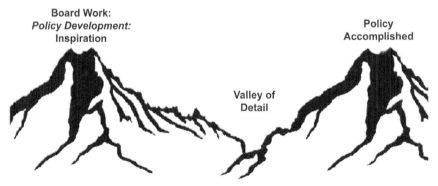

Mountain Peaks of Governance
Inspiring Creativity for a Policy

Board Work:
Policy Development:
Inspiration

**Policy
Accomplished**

**Valley of
Detail**

Figure 5.1.   Mountain Peaks of Governance: *Inspiring Creativity for a Policy. Source*: Copyright © 2016, Chuck Namit, Strategem LLC, Values Governance®

policy or goal. Developing and tracking a policy to its successful completion is a problem that faces most governance systems.

What to Do?

Here's the solution! The board sends the superintendent down into the valley of detail—school issues that must be resolved to accomplish the new policy. The superintendent then sends back monitoring reports to the board, as the issues are resolved. In effect, the monitoring reports to the board by the superintendent are similar to building pillars that support the sky bridge. With each monitoring report, a portion of the sky bridge is built so that the board, in an imaginary sense, avoids descending into the valley of detail—the superintendent's operational work (see figure 5.2).

Figure 5.2.   Mountain Peaks of Governance: *Monitoring to Create a Sky Bridge. Source*: Copyright © 2016, Chuck Namit, Strategem LLC, Values Governance®

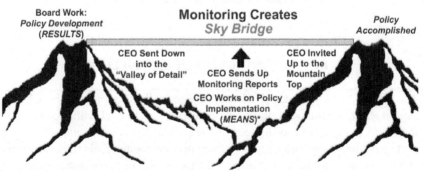

Figure 5.3.   Mountain Peaks of Governance: *Sky Bridge to Policy Completion. Source*: Copyright © 2016, Chuck Namit, Strategem LLC, Values Governance®

Now, why is this important? Many governance systems want board members to know their role but fail to provide a model or an approach to training board members. The Values Governance® system comes to grips with this issue. It modifies the monitoring concept by providing a sky bridge that monitors operational expectations that provides a safe path to travel for completion of the policy or other school district issues (see figure 5.3).

SKY BRIDGE SOLUTION TO GOVERNANCE LEADERSHIP

This allows a board to build a sky bridge through the monitoring process to reach its ends, results, or goals. The process follows these steps:

1. Policy development: The board—with the CEO close at hand—is charged with developing future policies.
2. CEO works on implementation of the policy: The board develops the policy, and the CEO is sent down into the valley of detail to prepare the work with the staff on the implementation of the policy.
3. Presentation of monitoring report: The CEO staff prepares periodic monitoring reports regarding various policies and sends them up to the board. See table 5.1 on page 36.

Figure 5.3 shows a division of roles—between the board and the CEO—that is important for a board and the CEO to know and appreciate. The roles—known as parallel leadership—include the following:

1. The board's role: The board provides guidance and direction setting for the organization to meet the owners' needs.
2. The CEO's role: The board sets the policy, and the CEO is figuratively sent down into the valley of detail to implement the policies through its operational expectations to reach the board's (and the organization's) results.

BOARD AND CEO ROLE CONFLICT

The phrase "valley of detail" is used allegorically to represent the CEO or superintendent being sent down into a deep valley to deal with the problems that need to be solved to implement the policy. However, some school districts have had board members—who do not understand their role—who also want to go into the valley to "help" the CEO do the implementation of policy job. In fact, consultants have observed that a board member who decides to go down into the valley of detail is really entering the valley of death because the board member will interfere with the CEO doing the job of implementation and responding to periodic monitoring reports.

MONITORING REPORTS: BOARD'S SKY BRIDGE TO POLICY COMPLETION

Board members—who do not understand the division of responsibility between the board and the CEO's roles—can cause conflict in the board-superintendent role. As the CEO works on the various issues that deal with the policy implementation, the board requires periodic monitoring reports. The monitoring report—in the illustration—is sent up for the board to examine if it is in compliance with the policy. When the monitoring report is in compliance, then allegorically it forms a sky bridge for the board to cross from the initial peak—that created the policy—to a future or distant peak, which represents the completed policy.

In summary, the sky bridge allows the board to cross over the bridge to reach the completed policy, without having to go down into the valley of detail, which is the CEO's domain.

Figure 5.3 on page 31 also shows important governance elements:

1. The governance team and the administrative team: The board usually invites the CEO (superintendent) and the administrative team to celebrate the completion of the policy.
2. Results: policy peak: The left peak is the starting point of the policy that is at the results level of governance.
3. Monitoring sky bridge: The board crosses the sky bridge—created by the monitoring reports—to reach the completed policy. The sky bridge keeps the board from descending into the valley of detail.
4. Valley of detail: This is the CEO work area, which develops the implementation and sends up monitoring reports to the board for its examination.

WHY USE ALLEGORIES?

Why do we use allegories to explain governance? For over sixty years, researchers have used the allegory of a window to establish the "Ohio State Quadrant or window model that describes various theories." Indeed, we've used the quadrant (or window model) and the bull's-eye circle model to describe the Policy Governance® and Coherent Governance® model.

In this chapter, we've used the visual elements of peaks and valleys to help us grasp some very complex concepts. In fact, the term "valley of death" is in the twenty-third Psalm. Simply put, allegory and stories provide a specific focus—author Peter Senge would call the Green-Line Clock a "mental model" that reminds us of the work that the board and the CEO must do to govern better.

MONITORING REPORTS: CHECK ON REACHING GOALS

John Carver developed the monitoring process in his Policy Governance® model. Later Dawson and Quinn carried forward the monitoring concept in their Coherent Governance® model. The Values Governance® system expands and enhances monitoring, identifying its role as the critical bridge to the accomplishment of a goal or a vital district process (e.g., boundary studies for schools).

Monitoring is one of the most innovative processes that can assist in governing an organization. Monitoring reports checks on the CEO's performance. The board uses the monitoring process to check the quality of content and adherence to board policy.

DEVELOPING THE MONITORING PROCESS

A vital step in governance process is to see how the quality of the work done is evaluated and is communicated to the board. The CEO must provide monitoring reports on the following:

1. The Goal Policies: The traditional governance model uses the word "goals," while Carver uses the term "ends policy," and Dawson and Quinn use the term "results policy." The Values Governance® goal is for the organization and CEO to make progress in reaching its goal policies. The efficiency of progress to goal achievement is tracked through monitoring reports as prepared by the CEO in performing his or her responsibilities as the executive.
2. Board-CEO Relationship Policies: The board examines the CEO's relationship with the board, as well as staff and owners.
3. Operational Expectations Policies: These are methods and techniques employed by the CEO to accomplish school district goals and include issues such as human relations, board communication, budget, financial administration, facilities, and asset protection.[1]

4. The Mountain Peak Model Design: The Values Governance® system clearly adds an important description in identifying the role models as each performs their tasks.

INCORPORATING THE MONITORING PROCESS IN THE TRADITIONAL GOVERNANCE MODEL

School districts that have adopted the alternative governance system have introduced a monitoring process to review school district programs that defines and uses the definitions of operational expectations (means) and results (ends) in their governance structure. These definitions are not defined or widely used in the traditional governance model; however, similar definitions could detail and evaluate the work of the board and CEO. The traditional governance model should incorporate the expanded and enhanced Values Governance® monitoring process.

The Values Governance® system provides vital ways to expand and improve the traditional governance model: multiple monitoring reports are used to evaluate the CEO and progress of the organization to meet a goal. For example: throughout the year, the board reviews multiple monitoring reports that provide specific points for evaluating the work of the CEO. The monitoring process also provides the board with many targeted opportunities to show the organization is achieving goals or results. It can also provide areas where improvement is indicated and must be enhanced.

The Values Governance® system has provided the Mountain Peaks of Governance and Monitoring Sky Bridge models that clearly describe the roles and expectations of the board and superintendent.

MONITORING REPORTS: SEVERAL LEVELS TO CONSIDER

The monitoring report should include the items in table 5.1.[2] Evidence in the monitoring report is provided to justify the progress and Edward deBono's method to identify interests while providing a cost versus benefit feature to the analysis. Although the monitoring reports are similar to progress reports in the traditional governance system, the multiple nature of the monitoring reports recommended by the Values Governance® system helps the board and the CEO to provide many points of evaluation and progress sharing.

Table 5.1.   Monitoring Report Form

1. Policy Statement: It must include a reasonable interpretation of the board policy.
2. Interpretation/Interest of the Policy: Included in the interpretation of the policy.
3. Use a decision-making tool developed by Edward deBono: I: Interpretation/interest = C: Cost versus B: Benefit
4. Evidence to Support the Interpretation/Interest: Demonstrate that reasonable progress indicates success by him or her.
5. Supporting Information and Data: Additional information/data to support the evidence.

Source: Modified from Edward deBono's thinking models of PMI = Plus, Minus, Interest and CAF = Considering All Factors

BOARD SELF-MONITORING

The Governance Culture (Process) policies and the Board-CEO Relationship policies—two of the four policy quadrants that make up the alternative governance models—are used by the board to monitor its performance. These types of policies should be included in the traditional governance system. The board must be in compliance with these policies. These monitoring reports will form the basis of the board self-assessment process we will discuss in chapter 6.

BOARD AND SUPERINTENDENT CONFLICT

Consultants frequently warn board members to stay out of the CEO's valley of detail because, for a board member, this will become the valley of death when it comes to good board-superintendent relations.

WHAT WE'VE LEARNED IN THE CHAPTER

Chapter theme: Creating an ongoing monitoring system—through a monitoring process—of the organization's culture, operational expectations, and results.

1. Under the Values Governance® system, the Mountain Peaks Governance and Monitoring Sky Bridge of Organizational Expectations is used by the board to check the quality of content and adherence to a policy. The board can check on the content in the ends/results policies, board-CEO

relationship policies, and the executive limitations/operational expectations (means) policies. The Values Governance® model provides this approach that uniquely defines the roles of the board and the superintendent in governing the school district.

2. The sky bridge allows the board to cross over the bridge to reach the completed policy, without having them descend into the valley of detail, which is the CEO's role or domain. Simply put, this process allows the board and CEO to remain in their appropriate domains—the board as governors and the CEO as a manager of the organization's operational expectations or means.

3. The traditional governance system can employ the modified monitoring process to augment and improve the governance process.

THE NEXT CHAPTER

In chapter 6, we will discuss the board and CEO relationship cycle that was developed by the Washington State School Directors' Association and is further developed by the Values Governance® system. These leadership functions are a board self-assessment instrument, developing and tracking a policy to completion, and a superintendent evaluation instrument that assure the community that the board and the superintendent are accountable for their leadership and performance.

More Advanced Information

As a new board member or a board member with some experience, you are not expected to read the more advanced information on the subject. However, at a later time, you can turn to chapter 15: Application-Opportunity C in the Field Manual.

Board and CEO Leadership: Board Self-Assessment and Superintendent Evaluation

---

Chapter challenge: How do we assess and evaluate the work of the board and the CEO?

Step 3: Values Governance® System

We will examine the board self-assessment and the superintendent evaluation instruments. We will also discuss the board and superintendent-CEO relationship accountability function to the public to assure school district leadership.

WE ASSESS STUDENTS, WHY NOT ASSESS AND EVALUATE THE BOARD AND CEO?

Over the years, the Washington State School Directors' Association (WSSDA) observed that school districts assess students for progress in the school district subject matter. Indeed, this author—and his consultants he worked with at the time—asked this question:

Why Don't We Assess Board Members and Evaluate Superintendents?

This author set the goal for his state association consultants: Develop techniques and instruments for an annual board self-assessment and superintendent evaluation to provide the community with assured accountability of the

)

school district leadership. We used the research on assessment and evaluation to formulate the following model: A school district-school board is the governance team and the superintendent leads the management team. Therefore, we raised these questions:

1. How does the school board track progress to goals?
2. How does the public know whether the board and superintendent are fulfilling their roles effectively?

One method of assessing the effectiveness of district leaders is an assessment and evaluation process. The self-assessment and evaluation measure progress and goal achievement. These tools provide the leadership team with the best opportunity to identify strengths and weaknesses.[1]

The Values Governance® system adopts the research developed by the WSSDA to use the board self-assessment and superintendent evaluation cycle in school districts that adopt its governance system.

EVALUATION VERSUS ASSESSMENT

It is important to differentiate between assessment and evaluation to more precisely define the function of each instrument. Ken O'Connor, the author of *How to Grade for Learning*, has provided some help. Although O'Connor's concepts for the assessment and the evaluation came from a grading frame of reference, we have adapted the concepts and applied them to the board self-assessment and superintendent evaluation process. An assessment is "the process of gathering information" about the school board's performance as it relates to the governance process and board-superintendent relations. It answers the question, "How is it going?"

An evaluation is "the process of integrating information from many sources and using it to make judgments" about the performance of the superintendent. It answers the question, "How good is it?" In effect, the board self-assesses its governance performance while evaluating the superintendent's performance in leading the school district. Ultimately, the public holds individual board members accountable for student success and the goals of the school district.[2]

During early 2000, the WSSDA unified the board self-assessment and superintendent evaluation model into a cycle of an integrated model of assessing the school district leadership.

Regardless of the criteria or standards that a school district chooses to use—in the traditional governance model or alternative governance models or Values Governance® model—the school district needs to develop a model of board self-assessment and superintendent evaluation. The model has a school board review its governmental process and consider how much their superintendent achieves and how he or she leads.

BOARD SELF-ASSESSMENT

The school board is primarily responsible for setting direction, for establishing policy, and for responding to the community in the area of governance. The self-assessment instrument has topics that deal with the work of the board in governance.

Here is a list of elements that should be in a board self-assessment instrument: One of the concepts in board self-assessment is to review the board's interaction with the superintendent under an element called the Board-Superintendent Relations (develops and maintains a relationship with superintendent):

1. Board-Community Relations. (Supports open dialogue with the community and local and state governmental leaders.)
2. Board-Instructional Programs Relations. (Provides oversight to revise, update, and monitor the instructional programs to improve student learning.)
3. Financial Management Monitoring. (Provides oversight for the district's financial condition.)
4. Policy Development. (Develops timely and appropriate policies to communication and community relations. Proactively engages and learns the community's expectations for the public schools.)
5. Board Meeting Effectiveness and Efficiency. (Encourages initiatives to improve the conduct and productivity of the school board meeting.)
6. Board Qualities. (Includes knowledge, independence, and respect for one another and decisions by the full board.)
7. Goal Setting and Planning. (Plans, develops, and implements appropriate goals.)
8. District Goals. (Evaluates and implements the global, board, and district operational goals.)[3]

Ranking the Board Self-Assessment Indicator Behavior

A typical board self-assessment topic is Board/Instructional Programs. The scoring for the indicator of the instrument has a five-point range that describes the board's behavior in governance. The five-point range starts with the following:

1. Behavior Description Indicators: To get you started, here are some examples of indicators: "Sets instructional goals," or "Cite new developments in curricula content." Now, using the examples as a guide, board members need to develop indicators for letters a through e.

    a. _____
    b. _____
    c. _____
    d. _____
    e. _____

2. Five-Point Ranking Scale: Each board member ranks the indicator from a number "1" as poor to "5" as superior.
3. Comments: Each board member can comment on the behavior and ranking.[4]

The bottom line of the self-assessment is to create conversation among the board, improving student achievement, and to assure the owners that the organization is meeting its goals (results, ends).

CEO OR SUPERINTENDENT EVALUATION

With the completion of the board self-assessment process, it is logical to look at evaluating the superintendent. In some states, it is a statutory requirement to evaluate the CEO or superintendent at least once annually.

Values Governance® system expands evaluation in the traditional governance CEO (Superintendent) Evaluation instrument so that it includes the elements listed on pages 42–43.

LEADERSHIP ELEMENTS

1. Strategic Direction:

    a. Ensures that the vision, mission, and district policy are aligned
    b. Offers professional recommendations based on best practices
    c. Administers district within policies of the board

2. Management of the District:

   a. Proactive leadership in improving the district
   b. Provides oversight of district operations
   c. Manages budgetary process

3. External Relations:

   a. Work proactively to build community support
   b. Develops legislative and regulatory relationships
   c. Works with public and private organizations

4. Leadership for Operation of District Programs:

   a. Keeps the board informed of progress toward goals
   b. Regulates district operations
   c. Provides the model for customer relations

5. Professional Qualities:

   a. Models the highest standards of performance
   b. Exercises exceptional judgment in decision making
   c. Communicates effectively with stakeholders and owners

6. Board Relationships:

   a. Treats board members with equal consideration and respect
   b. Keeps the board thoroughly informed on issues and needs
   c. Plans agenda with the board that results in an efficient meeting[5]

RANKING THE INDICATOR BEHAVIOR

The superintendent evaluation instrument has a five-point range that runs from a high-point of 5 to a low-point of 1. The five-point range starts with a Five-Point Ranking Scale. Each board member ranks the indicator from

a–b. Not meeting standard
c.   Progressing
d.   Proficient
e.   Exemplary

Comments: The person rating the performance can offer comments on Areas of Strength and Opportunities for Improvement.

   Program of Improvement: A program is established by the board to improve the performance of the CEO.[6]

TIMING OF THE BOARD SELF-ASSESSMENT
AND SUPERINTENDENT EVALUATION

The Values Governance® system clearly lays out a ten-step Process Cycle for Board Self-Assessment and Superintendent Evaluation (see figure 6.1).

At the beginning of the school year (June–July period), the board develops school district goals. Around January, the board conducts a mid-year

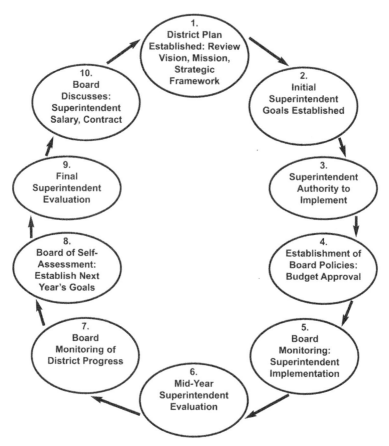

10-Step Process Cycle
Board Self-Assessment
& Superintendent Evaluation

1. District Plan Established: Review Vision, Mission, Strategic Framework

2. Initial Superintendent Goals Established

3. Superintendent Authority to Implement

4. Establishment of Board Policies: Budget Approval

5. Board Monitoring: Superintendent Implementation

6. Mid-Year Superintendent Evaluation

7. Board Monitoring of District Progress

8. Board of Self-Assessment: Establish Next Year's Goals

9. Final Superintendent Evaluation

10. Board Discusses: Superintendent Salary, Contract

Figure 6.1.   Ten-Step Process Cycle. *Source*: Copyright © 2016, Chuck Namit, Strategem LLC, Values Governance®

evaluation of the superintendent, which gives the superintendent a chance to apprise the board on progress to meeting goals. The midyear evaluation also provides the superintendent with the opportunity to modify goals because of circumstances that affect these goals. In May or June, the board conducts the final superintendent evaluation.

In March or April, the school board undertakes a board self-assessment of itself. The board's goal is to self-assess its governance process and practices, as well as review the board-superintendent relationship. Another part of the self-assessment process is to review the progress to achieving the district's

Board Self-Assessment and Superintendent Evaluation

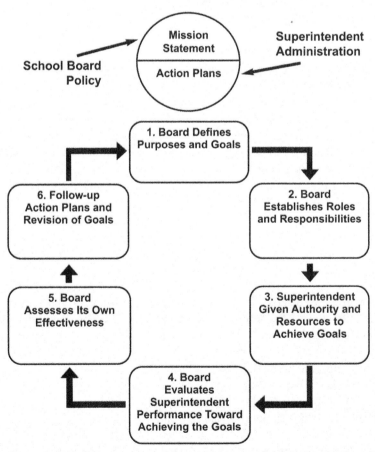

Figure 6.2.   Board Self-Assessment and Superintendent Evaluation. *Source*: Copyright © 2016, Chuck Namit, Strategem LLC, Values Governance®

goals for the current year and to plan for next year's goals.[7] The Values Governance® system board self-assessment and superintendent evaluation process clearly shows that the circle at the top of the model demonstrates the traditional governance model division of board's domain on the top part of the circle, while the administration or superintendent's domain is on the bottom (see figure 6.2).[8]

WHAT WE'VE LEARNED IN THE CHAPTER

Chapter theme: Evaluation and assessment of the organization's officers are accountability to stakeholders and owners.

1. The Values Governance® system adopts the research developed by the Washington State School Directors' Association (WSSDA) to use the board self-assessment and superintendent evaluation cycle in school districts that adopt its governance system.
2. The assessment process is gathering information about the organization or school district performance as it relates to the governance process. The stakeholders and owners receive the information from the school district. It answers the question, "How is it going?" In the board self-assessment process, we ask, "How well is the board doing?"
3. An evaluation is a process of integrating information from many sources, using board judgment and asking the question, "How good is it?" The board—in developing the superintendent evaluation—asks the question, "How good is he/she?"

THE NEXT CHAPTER

In chapter 7, we discuss the research of Karen L. Mapp on the four school-community stages of schools. This chapter identifies schools within the following categories:

1. The Fortress School (Below-Basic School)
2. The Come-If-We-Call School (Basic School)
3. The Open-Door School (Proficient School)
4. The Partnership School (Advanced School)

The chapter then provides a Values Governance® system that will score a school on trust, relationship, and the belief levels for each school that is rated.

More Advanced Information

As a new board member or a board member with some experience, you are not expected to read the more advanced information on the subject. However, at a later time, you can turn to chapter 16: Application-Opportunity D in the Field Manual.

Chapter 7

Four Phases of School-Community Engagement Stages

Chapter challenge: How can we judge the performance of schools? What can improve the learning of students in a school?

Step 4: Values Governance® System

We will review the ability to score schools on trust, relationship, and belief in schools. We will also discuss the research of Karen L. Mapp on the four school-community stages of schools. This chapter identifies schools within the following categories that are identified by Mapp:

1. Fortress School (Below-Basic School)
2. Come-If-We-Call School (Basic School)
3. Open-Door School (Proficient School)
4. Partnership School (Advanced School)

The number-one responsibility for the school board is to provide reliable, stable, and efficient schools for our students. Our citizens must believe that the schools are the best. This chapter provides a model to score a school on trust, relationship, and the belief levels for each school that is rated.

STUDENT EDUCATION IS THE KEY FUNCTION OF SCHOOLS

When the public discusses the importance of education in society, the answer typically is that education has the paramount duty to provide student growth, achievement, and the preservation of citizenship within our society. And in a similar fashion, the educational community—the board, administrators, teachers, and paraprofessionals—all want to deliver on the paramount duty of the community to the owners of the educational process.

Educational conferences—school board, administrators, and teacher groups—try to tie the two themes together: the public's goal, and the leader and professional commitment to improved student growth and achievement, and development of future citizens.

School districts want to demonstrate that their schools are successful and gain the public support of the community. Some schools, however, within a district, do not achieve at the same level. Parents and community seem to know which school is doing a better job of educating students.

At a recent school board conference, Mapp—an authority on school building performance and the school building relationship with the community—led a workshop. Mapp—a Harvard professor—shared her latest research on the four school-community engagement stages and school district practices.

RESEARCH ON SCHOOL-COMMUNITY ENGAGEMENT STAGES

As Mapp explored her research with the audience—the author sat at a table and drew a four-square window—placing Mapp's findings in each of the four windows. The author shared the approach with Mapp at the end of the presentation.

The four-square model—embedded with Mapp's research—highlighted the elements that separated unsuccessful schools with those that embraced the parents and the community. Mapp's research demonstrated the four school-community engagement stages. The key to building school-community engagement and partnerships is the development of school programs that "focus on building trusting and respectful relationships."[1]

Moreover, the belief in the school by parents and the community is essential to the success of the school. Parents, principal, staff, and the community tend to exhibit certain core beliefs in their school. These core beliefs include the following:

1. "Adopt the attitude that all families are involved in their children's education and want guidance in their efforts to support children's learning.
2. Encourage staff to implement both in-school and away-from-school initiatives."[2]

Let's Examine the Model

The model has four levels that distinguish the school attitude to the stakeholders and owners:

Stage 1: Fortress School (Below-Basic): The school is combative to the owners and stakeholders, with low trust, relationship, and belief in their schools.

Stage 2: Come-If-We-Call School (Basic): The school views itself as in containment to the owners and stakeholders, with a low-to-moderate trust, relationship, and belief in their schools.

Stage 3: Open-Door School (Proficient): The school seeks accommodation with the owners and stakeholders, with moderate trust, relationship, and belief in their schools.

Stage 4: Partnership School (Advanced):[3] The school sees itself in collaboration with the owners and stakeholders, with high trust, relationship, and belief in their schools.

EXPLANATION OF TABLE 7.1

The "School-Community Engagement Model" (see table 7.1) is a quadrant, with the upper part of the model describing the four stages of school development, based on Mapp's research.[4]

The four-square model—embedded with Mapp's research—will be used to demonstrate the four school-community engagement stages.

1. The Trust Level (T-1 to T-4) of your schools
2. The Relationship Level (R-1 to R-4) of your schools
3. The Belief Level (B-1 to B-4) of your schools

The information on your school districts is important from two points of view. First, the owners of the school district are vitally interested in how well the schools are doing and how the professionals view the data. Second, the important factors are the lower-level scores as well as the points of view of the school and staff (principals, teachers, aides, etc.). Again, you have only to go back and review the work to see how significant this information is in viewing your schools by the owners of the school district.

THE FOUR STAGES OF THE SCHOOLS

Mapp's research describes the four school stages—the Fortress (Below-Basic), Come-If-We-Call (Basic), Open-Door (Proficient), and Partnership (Advanced) as seen in table 7.1 on page 52. Mapp presented the research

Table 7.1.   School-Community Engagement Model*

Stage 3		Stage 2	
Open – Door *School (Proficient)*^ (Moderate *Trust*) (Moderate *Relationship*) (Moderate *Belief in School*)^B ATTITUDE ACCOMMODATION^C		*Come-If-We-Call* *School (Basic)*^ (Low-to-Moderate *Trust*) (Low-to-Moderate *Relationship*) (Low-to-Moderate *Belief in School*)^B ATTITUDE CONTAINMENT^C	
Stage 4		**Stage 1**	
Partnership *School (Advanced)*^ (High *Trust*) (High *Relationship*) (High *Belief in School*)^B ATTITUDE COLLABORATION^C		*Fortress* *School (Below-Basic)*^ (Low Trust) (Low Relationship) (Low Belief in School)^B ATTITUDE COMBATIVE^C	
T-4 (*High*) Trust Level	T-3 Trust Level	T-2 Trust Level	T-1 (*Low*) Trust Level
R-4 (*High*) Relationship Level	R-3 Relationship Level	R-2 Relationship Level	R-1 (*Low*) Relationship Level
B-4 (*High*) Belief Level	B-3 Belief Level	B-2 Belief Level	B-1 (*Low*)^B Belief Level

* *Note:* Karen L Mapp's research established four categories of schools, which included the following: Fortress School, Come-If-We Call School, Open-Door School, and Partnership School.

Source: Adapted from the research of Karen L. Mapp, *Moving Forward: Building the Capacity for Effective Family Engagement*, 2012. Copyright © 2016, Chuck Namit, Strategem LLC, Values Governance®

in a presentation at the Washington State School Directors' Association (WSSDA) annual conference.

The four stages of school-community engagement not only apply to a particular school building but apply equally to a school district as an organization.[5]

Stage 1: Fortress School: Below-Basic

This stage—based on the School-Community Engagement model shows a combative school attitude, with low trust, low relationship, and low belief level in the school among principal, staff, parents, and the community. This, in turn, foreshadows a frosty relationship between the school and its constituency.

These are some of the characteristics of Mapp's Fortress School:

1. Parents don't care about their children's education, and they are the main reason the kids are failing.

2. Parents don't come to conferences, no matter what we do.
3. Principal picks a small group of "cooperative parents to help out."
4. We're teachers, not social workers.
5. Curriculum and standards are too advanced for these parents.[6]

The critical factor in growing beyond this stage is whether the parties can begin to accept one another, by improving the trust capital of the relationship.

Stage 2: Come-If-We-Call School: Basic

This stage—based on the School-Community Engagement model—signifies a containment attitude, with low-to-moderate trust, low-to-moderate relationship, and low-to-moderate belief level in the school among principal, staff, parents, and the community. The best description of the relationship is an "armed truce." Both parties—parents/patrons and the school—realize the relationship will be a long one.

Some of the characteristics of Mapp's Come-If-We-Call School include the following:

1. Parents are told what students will be learning at the fall open house.
2. Workshops are planned by staff.
3. Families can visit [the] school on report card pickup day.
4. Parents call the office to get teacher-recorded messages about homework.[7]

The Come-If-We-Call School moderates its defensive attitude and rhetoric, but the suspicion of each other's motives is still very present.

Stage 3: Open-Door School: Proficient

This stage—based on the School-Community Engagement model—signifies an accommodation attitude, with a moderate trust, moderate relationship, and moderate belief level among principal, staff, parents, and the community.

Growing accommodation is the characteristic of this stage. The primary focus of the parties is to improve the relationship. Additionally, trust among the parties begins to develop.

Some of the characteristics of Mapp's Open-Door School include the following:

1. Parent-teacher conferences are held twice a year.
2. There is an "Action Team" for family engagement.
3. School holds parent events three or four times a year.
4. Parents raise issues at PTA meetings or see the principal.[8]

The attempt at improving the relationship has spawned a desire to achieve agreement using reason and persuasion. As the parties dialogue on the needs of students and the school, the focus moves to school problems and concerns.

Stage 4: Partnership School: Advanced

This stage—based on the School-Community Engagement model—signifies a collaboration attitude, with a high trust, high relationship, and high belief level in the school among staff, parents, and the community.

Moreover, this stage nurtures collaborative behavior that demonstrates open cooperation. The trust level is very high. The preferred way of dealing with one another is the problem-solving mode. The parties move from problem solvers to solution facilitators.

Some of the characteristics of Mapp's Partnership School include the following:

1. Families are seen as partners in improving educational outcomes.
2. All family activities connect to what students are learning.
3. There is a clear open process for resolving problems.[9]

Therefore, the demands, problems, and issues regarding the school are at a low level. A type of informal compact among parents, patrons, stakeholders, and the school is in place for day-to-day issues, which becomes the standard operating procedure.

The style of communication among the parties—the board and its stakeholders and owners—is open, honest, and frequent. Finally, the level of trust, depth of the relationship, and belief in the school evolve into an attitude and motto.

WHAT WE'VE LEARNED IN THE CHAPTER

Chapter theme: A board must understand the four school-community engagement stages and how it will support the stakeholders and owners.

1. Table 7.1 describes the four school-community engagement stages that board members must be aware of:
   a. The Fortress School (Below-Basic): The school attitude is combative in nature with low trust, relationship, and belief level among the staff, parents, and community.
   b. The Come-If-We-Call School (Basic): The school attitude shows a containment approach, with a low-to-moderate trust, relationship, and belief level among the staff, parents, and community.

c. The Open-Door School (Proficient): The school stage shows an accommodation attitude, with a moderate trust, relationship, and belief level among the staff, parents, and community.

d. The Partnership School (Advanced): The school stage shows a collaborative attitude, with high trust, relationship, and belief level among the staff, parents, and community.

The Values Governance® system believes that the School-Community Engagement model allows the community to gauge their schools in terms of the relationship, trust, and belief.

2. The board will undoubtedly want to use Karen L. Mapp's research on the four school-community engagement stages to examine each of their schools to see which window or stage the school fits.

THE NEXT CHAPTER

In chapter 8, we will examine the need to establish a research-based curriculum, which will help a school district to implement a curriculum that will do the following:

1. Provide the data needed to measure student progress
2. Increase student achievement
3. Provide all schools with systems needed to gain community support

The chapter will also deal with the reform issues that a school district must address:

1. How to put school reform and innovation into action
2. Review the various education initiatives that occur in the state and national scene

More Advanced Information

As a new board member or a board member with some experience, you are not expected to read the more advanced information on the subject. However, at a later time, you can turn to chapter 17: Application-Opportunity E in the Field Manual.

Chapter 8

School Governance and District Leadership to Increase Student Achievement

Chapter challenge: Students and their education are the main purpose or product of a school district. Therefore, this question must be answered: What are the roles of the board and the CEO?

Step 5: Values Governance® System

We recommend the adoption of a research-based or data-driven curriculum. We examine the need to implement a curriculum that will do the following:

1. Provide the data needed to measure student progress
2. Increase student achievement
3. Provide all schools with systems that are needed to gain community support

The chapter will also deal with the reform issues that a school district must address:

1. How to put school reform and innovation into action (strategic framework).
2. Review the various education initiatives that occur in the state and national scene.

The Values Governance® system believes that a board must assess the curriculum and instruction of its school district. These are the questions to ask:

1. Have our students met the standards of state assessments?
2. Do our graduates meet the school district mission?

3. Do all students have the academic and life skills necessary to succeed in a diverse world?

CURRICULUM CHANGE STARTS WITH A FIRM BOARD COMMITMENT TO ACCOUNTABILITY

Linda Dawson and Randy Quinn—in their book, *Good Governance Is a Choice*—raised the issue of "confused accountability." The question that must be answered to resolve this issue: Is that a decision of the school board or the CEO?

To answer this question, Dawson and Quinn pose this observation:

> The simple rule is: the party that makes the decision should be held accountable for the results of the decision.[1]

As Dawson and Quinn have stated in their simple rule, a school board must be committed and accountable for the result—improved student learning. So once a school district has examined its schools and determined a position on each school as determined by Karen L. Mapp's four stages of schools, the district must begin to examine a curriculum that is research based. This chapter will examine the need to establish a research-based curriculum, which will help a school district to implement a curriculum that will do the following:

1. Provide the data needed to measure student progress.
2. Increase student achievement.

IMPLEMENTING A RESEARCH-BASED CURRICULUM TO IMPROVE STUDENT LEARNING

The board must make the decision to move to a research-based curriculum and direct the CEO to pursue the curriculum.

A six-point outline will provide a planning guide for a board to study the adequacies of its curriculum. A board must take the governance position to initiate the movement to a new kind of research-based curriculum.

The following are steps that a school district must take to implement a research-based curriculum in a school district:

1. Board Initiates Research-Based Curriculum

Based on the North Thurston Public Schools (Washington) board delegation, the school district administration researched and presented an option regarding research-based curriculum. The board then hired a firm to do a complete horizontal and vertical audit of all schools, pointing out the strengths and weaknesses of each school, administration, and staff. The firm then makes recommendations and provides training.[2]

2. Research-Based Consulting Firm Conducts a School District Audit and Subsequent Training

Indeed, we live in an era in which the entire country is discussing education reform. Therefore, it is important for a school board to examine and discuss a research-based curriculum. The consulting firm offered the following deliverables:

a. Complete a professional assessment of the school district
b. Give a recommendation for creating benchmark assessments
c. Provide consulting services that focus on leadership training:

—Professional development
—Communication to the board, administration, staff, and community
—Evaluation of program and progress of implementation
—Monitoring of the program[3]

3. Engage Staff in the Research-Based Curriculum

The engagement of staff—principals and teachers—in the development of the research-based curriculum is critical. Choosing a research-based curriculum is done through the professional development process. The North Thurston Public Schools selected the Effective Schools model of the research-based curriculum. The professional development takes the form of the following techniques: data teams, professional learning communities, reflective practices, and continuous improvement.[4]

The district wants to create teacher champions or ambassadors to support the research-based curriculum with the principal and teacher engagement. It is also an important concept that the district gains the support of the teacher association, which in some states is similar to a union that represents the educational employees. It is also critical to have the support of the principals' organization if there is one in your district.

4. Report on the Audit Results

The consulting firm will report the results of the school district audit, showing the strengths and weaknesses of each school, administration, and staff. The report will also recommend the strategic direction that the board must discuss and pass on its direction for the school district.

5. Response to the Audit Results: The Newspaper Editorial

The staff, community, and city newspaper are presented with the audit results and conclusions.

"The audit gives North Thurston clear direction on what is working and what is not. The next step is to make the systemic changes that were recommended in the audit. That's not an easy task, but it's one the district must pursue. Administrators must put a plan together that will keep all the partners in the North Thurston District rowing in the same direction."[5]

6. Preparing the Staff to Implement the Research-Based Curriculum

After the research-based curriculum audit, the board delegated to the superintendent that he should begin to work with school district staff to implement the curriculum to improve the performance of the students. The implementation of a curriculum program will take several years. The important task is for the school board and the administration to "keep all the partners . . . rowing in the same direction" (Jim Koval, superintendent).[6]

FUTURESCAPE: A SCHOOL DISTRICT DEVELOPMENT OF A RESEARCH-BASED CURRICULUM AND STRATEGIC FRAMEWORK

With the selection of the superintendent in 2009—Raj Manhas—the board chose a person who would continue the change in the school district. The superintendent—under the board's direction—developed a new strategic framework to continue the change within the school district.

The school district implemented programs that would enhance the development of the research-based curriculum. The strategic framework was designed to improve student learning and develop financial stability in the school district while developing a new culture of compassion for the school district and the community. The school district developed many programs around the six strategic focus areas:

1. Make student learning the center of everything we do
2. Support the needs of the whole child
3. Strengthen community engagement to support student learning
4. Develop a trusting work culture through effective leadership and communication
5. Be fiscally accountable and efficient in the use of public resources
6. Ensure that the board and the superintendent develop an annual set of school district goals[7]

CHANGE IN LEADERSHIP IS CONSTANT

Change in district leadership continues in every school system. And so it is with our case study of the North Thurston Public Schools. The school district recently selected a new superintendent. As the new superintendent, Dr. Debra Clemens stated to the staff and community that the school district "begins this journey . . . to create a bright future for all our students."

WHAT WE'VE LEARNED IN THE CHAPTER

Chapter theme: A board's chief responsibility is to create an efficient governing system that improves student learning and achievement.

In the last chapter, a model was given to gauge the schools in the school district. It then seems to follow: Why do you serve on your board? Many answer this question in this fashion: To improve a student's achievement in our schools.

School districts can implement programs used with the strategic framework model. These programs that improve student learning and community engagement programs grow a trusting school district staff and develop a compassionate community culture.

A six-point outline of the strategic focus areas assists a school board in implementing a research-based curriculum to improve the curriculum while raising student achievement. Equally important is the development of a strategic framework leadership model.

THE NEXT CHAPTER

Chapter 9 offers the board the opportunity to develop its own beliefs, community values, and principles that define their governance for the school district.

More Advanced Information

As a new board member or a board member with some experience, you are not expected to read the more advanced information on the subject. However, at a later time, you can turn to chapter 18: Application-Opportunity F in the Field Manual.

Chapter 9

Establishing a Communication Style and Policy Control Status for Your Governance

> Chapter challenge: How can we gauge the depth of control that the board must have in directing the school district to meet the owners' expectations?

Step 6: Values Governance® System

The board needs to formulate the basis for developing a new governance process by establishing a policy control status of the board to determine whether the board is task-focused, moderate, or relationship-focused in developing school district policies. The school board members will also be able to determine their communication styles while connecting more effectively with the owners of the organization.

KEY AREA 1—LEARNING YOUR POLICY CONTROL STATUS

To determine the board's policy control status, each board member must work with two instruments:

1. Communication Style Survey (a Myer-Briggs look-alike exercise)
2. Governance Profile Scale

Communication Style

There are several communication instruments in business and service organizations that help you understand what controls your communication behavior.

64 Chapter 9

A communication instrument that provides you with a view of your communication style—that simulates the Myers-Briggs communication instrument—is called the Communication Style Survey.

The result of the Communication Style Survey can help board members and the superintendent or CEO understand their communication and behavior styles. Typically, board members have different styles. The bottom line of the communication instrument is this:

It is not the purpose of the instrument to try to control one another, but learn that each person has a different communication style, and you are trying to work together as a team—a board—by learning each other's style.[1]

Communication Style Survey

Directions: To help you identify your communication style, circle the word or phrase in each of the pairs that appeals to you most. See table 9.1. Don't think about your answer: let your first impression control your choice.

Communication Style Answer Sheet

Directions: Now transfer your answers from each of the sixteen pairs onto the answer sheet. See table 9.2. Using the answer key, see how many answers you had for sensor (S), intuition (I), thinker (T), and feeler (F). Enter your

Table 9.1. Communication Style Survey

1. A. Pragmatic	B. Creative Thinker
2. A. Sentimental	B. Introverted
3. A. Innovative	B. Concrete
4. A. Methodical	B. Impromptu
5. A. Thought-Provoking	B. Qualified
6. A. Stable	B. Congenial
7. A. New Ideas	B. Implementer
8. A. Nostalgic	B. Logical
9. A. Realistic	B. Visionary
10. A. Commanding	B. Ardent
11. A. Futuristic	B. Trustworthy
12. A. Passionate	B. Laid Back
13. A. Out-of-the-Box Thinking	B. Sense of Duty
14. A. Call the Shots	B. Motivator
15. A. Explicit	B. All-encompassing
16. A. Merciful	B. Logical

Source: Adapted material from "Find Out How Your Journal Personality May Be at Odds," *Working Smart,* The Executive Service from Learning International, vol. 3, no. 1, January 1986. Copyright © 2016, Chuck Namit, Strategem LLC, Values Governance®

Table 9.2. Communication Style Answer Sheet

1.	A (S)	B (I)		9.	A (S)	B (I)	
2.	A (F)	B (T)		10.	A (T)	B (F)	
3.	A (I)	B (S)		11.	A (I)	B (S)	
4.	A (T)	B (F)		12.	A (F)	B (T)	
5.	A (I)	B (S)		13.	A (I)	B (S)	
6.	A (T)	B (F)		14.	A (T)	B (F)	
7.	A (I)	B (S)		15.	A (S)	B (I)	
8.	A (F)	B (T)		16.	A (F)	B (T)	
Intuition (I)			Thinker (T)	Sensor (S)			Feeler (F)

scores in the spaces. The total score (sensor + intuition + thinker + feeler) must add up to sixteen.

Interpreting Your Communication Style Survey Score

Your highest score will indicate your dominant communication style. The next highest score will indicate your secondary communication style (see table 9.3).

A communication instrument is used by most organizations to determine the communication style of their employees. The Myers-Briggs instrument grew out of the work of psychologist Carl Jung. Jung's work was used in World War II to deal with soldiers and their perceptions of themselves and the world.

The elements in table 9.3 break down as follows:

- Italicized type is the Communications Style Survey instrument language that simulates the Myers-Briggs instrument (e.g., intuition).
- Under each of the styles you'll note its characteristics (e.g., directive, energetic), which will give you further insight into the style.

After each board member completes the Communication Style Survey instrument, it is time to review the Communication Style (see table 9.3).[2]

The communication windows determine the elements that describe an individual's type of communication.

Each board member must complete the Communication Style Survey. The instrument breaks down the various behavior and communication styles into four styles: intuition, thinker, feeler, and sensor. It also identifies communication and behavioral characteristics, potential strengths, and weaknesses. The

Table 9.3. Communication Style

	RELATIONSHIP FOCUS		
A S S E R	*Intuition*[2a] Characteristics: • **Directive** • **Energetic**	*Feeler*[2b] Characteristics: • **Congenial** • **Judicious**	C O O P E R
T I V E	*Sensor*[2c] Characteristics: • **Determinative** • **Purposeful**	*Thinker*[2d] Characteristics: • **Investigative** • **Organized**	A T I V E
	TASK FOCUS		

Source: Adapted material from "Find Out How Your Journal Personality May Be At Odds," *Working Smart,* The Executive Service from Learning International, vol. 3, no. 1, January 1986. Copyright © 2016, Chuck Namit, Strategem LLC, Values Governance®

Communication Style Survey allows each board member to compare and discuss their position on the instrument. It also will allow each board member to reflect on their style and behavior about the board's work, such as dealing with the superintendent, staff, parents, and the broader community.

Governance Profile Scale (GPS)[3]

The communication windows determine the elements that describe an individual's type of communication. The next instrument—Governance Profile Scale (GPS)—allows a board member to establish his or her governance preference toward policies that are task-focused, moderate, or relationship-focused.

Directions: The subject of each question is a board member skill. Each member of the board will take this survey and role-play that they are "the chair"; therefore, do the following in answering the question: Under each question, choose a statement (A, B, or C); be very honest with your answers; and score the statement based on your performance as chair with "1" being "Task-Focused" through "10" being "Relationship-Focused." The test begins on page 67. Score your results on page 68.

Count Governance Profile Scale (GPS) Score[4]

Count the numbers in each of the ten questions and list the total score: Total Governance Profile Scale (GPS) score: _____

Now, on the scale, list your Governance Profile Scale (GPS) and identify your tendency toward relationship-focused, moderate, or task-focused policy

GPS TEST SCALE

Choose A, B, or C; then circle the number that describes your approach to that choice.

1. When it comes to setting board goals with other school board members, as Chair, I:
___ A Set my own goals and try to convince other board members regarding the merits of the goals.
___ B Allow each of the other board members to set their own goals.
___ C See my role as balancing the board's needs and the community's needs.

1	2	3	4	5	6	7	8	9	10
Task-Focused				Moderate			Relationship-Focused		

2. In organizing the work of the school board, as Chair, I:
___ A See my role as balancing the board's needs and the community's needs.
___ B Believe board members must commit their time and talents to overcome challenges facing the district.
___ C Match board members who have interest in their board work.

1	2	3	4	5	6	7	8	9	10
Task-Focused				Moderate			Relationship-Focused		

3. In assessing the school board's performance issues, as Chair, I:
___ A Observe other member's performance and tell them how to improve.
___ B Give positive feedback to help member performance.
___ C Measure a member's performance against an agreed-upon standard.

1	2	3	4	5	6	7	8	9	10
Task-Focused				Moderate			Relationship-Focused		

4. When selecting a new school board member, as Chair, I look for a person who:
___ A Will add new skill(s) to our board.
___ B Displays a collaborative nature, and "plays well with others."
___ C Can "hit the ground running."

1	2	3	4	5	6	7	8	9	10
Task-Focused				Moderate			Relationship-Focused		

5. When authorizing expenditure of funds and/or time for training school board members, as Chair, I:
___ A Extend training that leads to harmony on the board.
___ B Support the needed training to develop the board.
___ C Take direct responsibility for training that will benefit the board.

1	2	3	4	5	6	7	8	9	10
Task-Focused				Moderate			Relationship-Focused		

6. When I give direction to the superintendent–at the behest of the school board–as Chair, I:
___ A Require the superintendent to respect the board's position and obey the direction.
___ B Get the superintendent's ideas on issues, then relay the board's direction to the superintendent.
___ C Give board's direction to the superintendent buttressed by policy.

1	2	3	4	5	6	7	8	9	10
Task-Focused				Moderate			Relationship-Focused		

7. When delegating authority and responsibility to other school board members, as Chair, I:
___ A Keep the authority to delegate responsibility to the appropriate individual.
___ B Delegate the appropriate authority to individual members based on their skills and abilities.
___ C Match my delegation based on the willingness to accept the responsibility.

1	2	3	4	5	6	7	8	9	10
Task-Focused				Moderate			Relationship-Focused		

8. When a school board member violates our board Operating Procedures or a district policy, as Chair, I:
___ A Use personal counseling to head off board disciplinary action.
___ B Try to nip bad behavior as soon as possible
___ C Work with board members to rehabilitate personal behavior and self-esteem.

1	2	3	4	5	6	7	8	9	10
Task-Focused				Moderate			Relationship-Focused		

9. When there is conflict (between members, between board and superintendent), as Chair, I:
___ A Resolve conflict by the two parties working out a solution.
___ B Get facts and reason for the conflict to find a solution.
___ C Rely on the board's sensitivity to each other to resolve the conflict.

1	2	3	4	5	6	7	8	9	10
Task-Focused				Moderate			Relationship-Focused		

10. When communicating with school board members and the superintendent, as Chair, I:
___ A Prefer to communicate interpersonally.
___ B Prefer to put my thoughts in writing to be understood.
___ C Rely on continuous open, honest communication about all board and district issues.

1	2	3	4	5	6	7	8	9	10
Task-Focused				Moderate			Relationship-Focused		

Figure 9.1–9.3. GPS Test Scale. *Source*: Copyright © 2016, Chuck Namit, Strategem LLC, Values Governance®

development. If your number is not precisely listed, modify the nearest number to fit your Governance Profile Scale scale/score.

Scoring the Governance Profile Scale (GPS)

Directions: List your Governance Profile Scale score. Once your GPS number is placed in the number column, you can then identify your "tendency toward" relationship-focused, moderate, or task-focused policy development. If your number is not precisely listed, modify to the nearest number to fit your GPS scale/score.

- **RELATIONSHIP FOCUSED POLICIES: TENDENCY TOWARD (Numbers 51 to 100)**

  100 ____ 95 ____ 90 ____ 85 ____ 80 ____

  75 ____ 70 ____ 65 ____ 60 ____ 55 ____ 51 ____

- **MODERATE POLICIES: TENDENCY TOWARD (Numbers 36 to 50)**

  50 ____ 45 ____ 40 ____ 36 ____

- **TASK FOCUSED POLICIES: TENDENCY TOWARD (Numbers 10 to 35)**

  35 ____ 30 ____ 25 ____ 20 ____ 10 ____

Figure 9.4. GPS Score. *Source*: Copyright © 2016, Chuck Namit, Strategem LLC, Values Governance®

List actual GPS score: _____.
List policy tendency (relationship-focused, moderate, or task-focused): _____.

KEY AREA 2—COMMUNICATION AND GOVERNANCE STYLES

These two instruments help a board member understand the elements that control his or her work and governance behavior. So let's review the instruments. First, the Communication Style Survey allows each board member to compare and discuss their position on the instrument. Second, the Governance Profile Scale differentiates between the relationship and the task-oriented behavior.[5]

In summary, the Governance Profile Scale (GPS) instrument will give you a good idea of your style, whether you are task-focused, moderate, or relationship-focused as indicated in your governance style in policy development.

A Skilled Consultant Can Be Useful

A final thought: Many times the use of a skilled consultant or facilitator can be useful in the discussion about an individual board member's GPS and the determination of the board's GPS.

Bull's-Eye Approach: Establishing Policy Control Status

The board can use the bull's-eye approach that makes the board feel more comfortable with the policies and the degree of control. Specifically, it's a way to think of the layering of policies. An example of a bull's-eye will be used to indicate the degrees of policy control. Each policy layer—as you move toward the center of the bull's-eye—represents a higher level of control (see figure 9.5).

The bull's-eye has two functions. First, imagine the arrow gauge at the bottom of the model, which shifts the degree of control, with the maximum degree of control by the board as you move to the center of the bull's-eye. Second, the reverse is also true: specifically, the board, at some subsequent time, reduces its control over a policy area by eliminating policies and moves to the outer ring (away from the center of the bull's-eye). Each policy can—and frequently does—have a different degree of control and scrutiny, which provides the CEO with degrees of flexibility and freedom to use any means (operational expectations) to implement the policy. Within any of the four policy areas of the model, the complex policy work of the board often graphically resembles a bull's-eye pattern.

The bull's-eye model of your policy control is a measure of your board members' personal behavior. Here are examples of the policy control rings' status:

1. Inner Ring: Task-focused policy control ring
2. Middle Ring: Moderate policy control ring
3. Outer Ring: Relationship-focused policy control ring

The Values Governance® system has adapted Carver's model to depict the board's Rings of Control approach.[6]

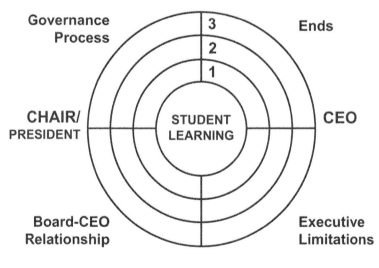

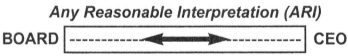

Figure 9.5.   Rings of Control Determined by the Board through Any Reasonable Interpretation. *Source*: Adapted material from John Carver and Miriam Mayhew Carver, *Reinventing Your Board* (Jossey-Bass Inc., 1997). Copyright © 2016, Chuck Namit, Strategem LLC, Values Governance®

If there is a dispute over the board's policy control status (GPS), answer this question: Given all the board members' work on the GPS instrument, what is the board's consensus of the policy control status? Is the policy control status—set in the type of policies—set at (1) task-focused, (2) moderate, or (3) relationship-focused? Therefore, the board—based on reviewing the board members' GPS scores—must come together in agreement and establish the board's policy control status for the school district: task-focused, moderate, or relationship-focused.

What We've Learned in the Chapter

Chapter theme: The board's role is to establish its values and policy control status for a new governance system.

1. The bull's-eye element of your policy controls model is a measure of your board members' political and personal behavior that determines whether your board is a task-focused, moderate, or relationship-focused policy board.
2. How do you determine your policy control status? Each board member can complete two different instruments (the communications instruments and the governance instruments) that will determine the board member's communication and Governance Profile Scale (GPS). Then, the fun begins when the board determines their overall board governance style.

THE NEXT CHAPTER

In chapter 10, the missing element is a method to Energize the Community process. It is a way that the board uses to provide information to all community and business leaders, as well as parent groups regarding the following:

1. What is the achievement level of our students?
2. How can community/business leaders work with the schools to help shape success and correct problems?
3. What programs or resources are needed to improve/assure student success?

The board—in this intensified process—is a balance among parents, community, and business leader invitees. Schools should open up to the community and businesses. The school district needs to be a source of guidance to the business and other agencies on what they could do to help students succeed.

More Advanced Information

As a new board member or a board member with some experience, you are not expected to read the more advanced information on the subject. However, at a later time, you can turn to chapter 19: Application-Opportunity G (strengths and weaknesses of intuition, thinker, sensor, and feeler) and chapter 20: Application-Opportunity H (Governance Profile Scale helps a board determine their policy control status) in the Field Manual.

Chapter 10

Energizing Community Engagement in Two-Way Governance

Chapter challenge: How do we engage in two-way listening and communication processes with the owners of our schools?

Step 7: Values Governance® System

The board uses the community engagement process and the two-way linkage meetings to keep in touch with the school district owners. The Values Governance® system provides the missing element that is a method to energize the community engagement process. It is a way that the board uses to provide information to all the community—parent and nonparent groups—and business leaders.

Moreover, the public schools need to open up to the community and businesses. The school district needs to be a source of guidance to the businesses and other agencies on what is required to help students succeed.

Finally, when the board adds the Energizing/Compelling Process to the Linkage Process, it also provides the secret to full governance in the school district.

GETTING IN SYNC WITH THE OWNERS OF YOUR ORGANIZATION

One of the most important parts of a board's job is to stay in communication with the owners and stakeholders. John Carver—in the Policy Governance® model—originally introduced the concept of linkage meetings with the owners and stakeholders, and Dawson and Quinn extended the linkage concept with more extensive dialogue meetings that are deliberate and consistent.[1] The refocused dialogue meeting sessions are created to "build mutually supportive relationships between the board and its owners and stakeholders," and strengthen the relationship between the board and the community to achieve the board's results (goals).[2]

The Values Governance® system believes that board members must add the missing method of energizing the community in the work of the school district. It is the way that the board uses to provide information to all community, stakeholders, and business leaders, as well as parent groups regarding the following:

1. What is the achievement level of our students?
2. How can community/business leaders work with the schools to help shape success and correct problems?
3. What programs/resources are needed to improve/assure student success?

LINKING THE LISTENING AND ENERGIZED PROCESSES

If the school district is a small organization, the listening process (linkage-dialogue processes) and energized community process (community engagement approaches) can be simpler. However, if the organization is a large one, then the listening process and the energized community process can be more sophisticated in its approach. Whether the organization is a large or small one, "walk the talk" of the governance model by looking at your "goals" or "results" policies to determine the purpose, mission, and focus.

Now, let's look at the listening and energized community processes.

A VISUAL VIEW OF THE LINKAGE PROCESS[3]

As we've mentioned before, the school board's role in governance is vital to the success of leading the school district. Although governance models claim to discuss the full role of the board, many provide only half of the board's responsibilities. In the traditional method of describing a typical school board, the community elects trustees to represent them in running the schools. An organization chart shows the community at the top with elected representatives sitting on a board. They would hire a superintendent who operates the schools. See figure 10.1 for an illustration of the board's governance structure.

A Board's Relationship
With Community and Schools

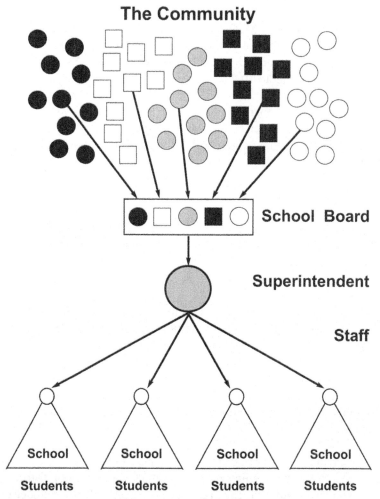

Figure 10.1. A Board's Relationship with Community and Schools. *Source*: Adapted from a Chuck Namit and Bob Hughes' article: www.district.com/article/energizing-engagement-community-governance, 2014. Copyright © 2016, Chuck Namit, Strategem LLC, Values Governance®

The Values Governance® system provides high-performing community engagement techniques and approaches that provide board members with tools that develop a full two-way governance in Chapter Application-Opportunity I on page 173.

Most people would argue that school board members should represent the entire community. However, a board member could belong to a special interest. The goal, of course, is to work with the school board so that the board members pledge to represent the entire community.

1. The Linkage Process. Many governing models listen to the community. Specifically, the alternative governance systems—mentioned in chapter 2—have a method called the "Listening Linkage Process," which is demonstrated in figure 10.2.

It is a way that the board uses to listen and, therefore, funnel the information from the public or community to the board and administration to provide direction to the school district regarding the education of their children.

2. The Missing Role of the Board in Governing: Energizing the Community Process. The Linkage Process—for most board members—is the only community involvement. However, this is only half of the board's role. The missing element is a process to energize the community. It is a way that the board uses to provide information to all community and business leaders, as well as parent groups. See figure 10.3 to see how the process works.
3. Introducing the Two-Way Full Linkage Process: Listening to the Community While Compelling Community/Business Leader Engagement. The alternative governance systems have a "Linkage Process" that requires governing officers (the board) to listen to the community as a gauge to see how well the school district is performing in educating the students. Scheduling regular linkage meetings with community/business leaders does this. This is very important because the board is asking for feedback from the leaders.

However, to make school district governance a success, you need to add something more than mere linkage process. To this end, school districts need to employ a Two-Way Full Linkage Process. Specifically, the model would include two elements to the process:

Process Element 1: Listening Inquiry Linkage: Regular meetings with parents and the community/business leaders are scheduled to ask for the leaders to give their feedback on how well the school district is doing in examining problems, and challenging and educating the students. The board must ask the parents and community/business leaders many probing questions that attempt to (1) see the problems students are experiencing, (2) identify the challenges

Listening Linkage Process

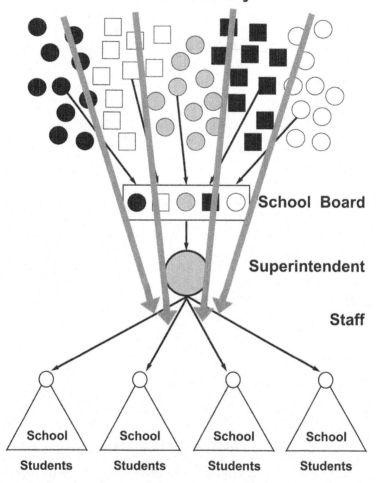

The downward-facing arrows reflect the communication from the
Community to the Board through the Board's Listening Linkages.

Figure 10.2. A Board's Relationship with Community and Schools. *Source*: Adapted
from a Chuck Namit and Bob Hughes' article: www.district.com/article/energizing-
engagement-community-governance, 2014. Copyright © 2016, Chuck Namit, Strategem
LLC, Values Governance®

Energize the Community Process

The Community

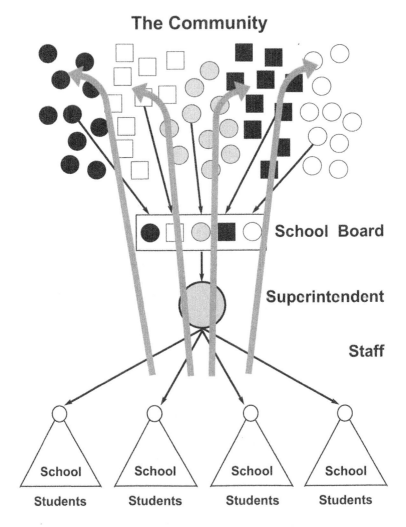

The upward-facing arrows reflect the Board and the Administration/Staff engaging the Community for assistance in educating Students.

Figure 10.3.   Energize the Community Process. *Source*: Adapted from a Chuck Namit and Bob Hughes' article: www.district.com/article/energizing-engagement-community-governance, 2014. Copyright © 2016, Chuck Namit, Strategem LLC, Values Governance®

that are needed, and (3) ensure that student successes within the schools are acknowledged.

The board—in this intensified process—must make sure that the invitees to the process are an even number of parents and community/business leaders.

Process Element 2: Energize and Compel the Community/Business Leaders to Engage Students to be Successful: The board—with the assistance of the administration—needs to challenge the community/business leaders to become engaged, and thereby compel them to help students be successful.

The second process element—Energize and Compel the Community/Business Leaders to Engage Students to be Successful—is a much different role than many school district boards see as their role in governance. The Two-Way Full Linkage Process completes a school district governance model that is not present in most governance models.

THE ELEMENTS TO ENERGIZE
THE COMMUNITY PROCESS[4]

Once a board has received information through the listening inquiry linkage, the board must "flip the process" by performing the Energize the Community Process. Specifically, the board must identify a list of "special audiences," as well as "identifying the source" of the audience. These special audiences include the groups listed in table 10.1.

Once the board has identified the "special audiences," it is the board and administration's responsibility to provide a series of activities that allow the board and the administration to speak with their true constituency: utilizing the following model by the community.

Table 10.1.   Board & Administration Interact With Special Audiences

Special Audiences	Identifying the Source
Elected Leaders	Legislators, City Council, Mayor, County Council, County Executive
Appointed Leaders	Park Board, City Managers, Fire Chief, Police Chief
Recognized Leaders	Clergy, Chamber of Commerce, Business Groups
Support Organizations	Boys & Girls Club, Homeless, Food Bank, Senior Centers, PTSA, Foundations
Ethnic Groups	Indian/Alaska Native, Pacific Islander, Asian, Black/African American, Hispanic, etc.

Source: Adapted from an article of Chuck Namit and Bob Hughes: www.district.com/article/energizing-engagement-community-governance, 2014. Copyright © 2016, Chuck Namit, Strategem LLC, Values Governance®

SCHOOLS SHOULD "OPEN UP" TO THE DISTRICT
COMMUNITY AND BUSINESSES[5]

Most recently, schools have sought partnerships with various agencies. These partnerships are a kind of a sharing for mutual benefit, which is a "give and take" proposition. For example—to be in a business partnership—a school district receives something of value from the business and gives something back in return. But in a typical partnership relationship, something is missing. Simply put, the partnership is usually just centered on a business gift to the school. Obviously, the solution by the school district is to expand this relationship.

What can the school district do to help students succeed? Simply put, the school district needs to put itself in the shoes of a business or community agency CEO. Since the executives—through various partnership programs— have given the schools a value (cash, products, employee time, etc.), the school district, in turn, could thank the business or community agency for their support, thereby engendering the goodwill of the community to the business or community agency for their gifts.

Schools need to open up to the community and businesses. The school district should be a source of guidance to the business and other agencies on what they could do to help students succeed. Here's how it would work:

1. Develop a public enterprise.
2. Modify the school curriculum to raise student awareness of businesses and civic organizations.
3. Make sure the schools are open and welcoming to community agencies and businesses.

Here are three ways actually in use by different boards to help and assist businesses and civic organizations in the work that they do.

- Development of a public enterprise: The Cedar River Academy Middle School in Washington State is a private school. According to school officials, students have established long-range learning projects that used student ideas, suggestions, and recommendations for the city of Enumclaw's redesign of Mahler Public Park.
- Development of a GRAVITY (School to Reengage Students and to Assist Businesses): The GRAVITY Consortium Reengagement Program in Washington State was started at the Educational Service District (ESD) 113. Students resolve local business problems; for example, a business recently expressed concern about a stack of tires—which tend to draw water in a wet environment—that could cause a health hazard. The students were then

challenged to design a solution to assist the business in dealing with the situation. Here are possible solutions—recommended to students by a board member—to deal with discarded automobile tires to avoid possible disease through mosquito infestation: (1) anchor the tires together with chains, (2) sink tires into a river or ocean bay, and (3) create a skin-diving park for divers.

- Modifying the school curriculum to raise student awareness of businesses and civic organizations: In another vein, the school district curriculum could also emphasize to students that they could be a future employee of a business or community agency. For example, the students discuss their future role in a business or a community agency. Here's how it could work: The school district curriculum—through a DECA Class Study—could emphasize the role of business in developing a sample marketing campaign for a nonprofit or a for-profit company. Business executives could then be brought into the classroom to discuss with the students the strategies for the implementation of the sample program and the effect the campaign would have on the community. The by-product of this kind of study emphasizes to the students the possibility of a future business career and the skills needed to be successful.[6]

THE TWO-WAY LINKAGE PROCESS PROVIDES FULL GOVERNANCE[7]

Typically, a school board provides only the Listening Linkage Process—a governance element that is passive—with the board listening to community/business/workplace leaders. It is, in effect, providing only half of the full governance role. But, when you add the Energizing/Compelling Process to the Linkage Process, the board becomes active—since it is speaking with and to the community/business/workplace leaders by asking for input on (1) "what needs to happen" in the schools, (2) how to "work with the schools" to help students, and (3) how to "correct the problems."

The Two-Way Linkage Process provides the board and the school district with another important advantage. It is important that a school district needs to understand the 30/70 paradox of community population. For example, typically a school district will spend an enormous amount of energy in serving 30 percent of the community population that has children in the district. But, the Two-Way Linkage Process continues to allow the school district to serve the 30 percent of the community that has students in the district, while simultaneously allowing the school district to focus on the 70 percent of the population that do not have students in the school district.

TWO-WAY COMMUNICATION BETWEEN OWNERS AND THE ORGANIZATION IS THE SECRET TO FULL GOVERNANCE[8]

Finally, the Two-Way Linkage Process works equally well with the traditional governance structures and the alternative governance systems—the Policy Governance® and Coherent Governance® models.

In effect—through the use of the Values Governance® system—the Two-Way Linkage Process is the full two-way governance system that is needed to have effective schools and improve school governance for the entire community.

What We've Learned in the Chapter

Chapter theme: The board's role in governance is to add to the Listening Linkage process, an energized community process that fully engages the community in what we have called a full two-way governance system.

1. Although a Listening Linkage process provides an organizational listening process, the missing element is a method to energize the community. It is a way that the board uses to provide information to all community and business leaders, as well as parent groups regarding:

    a. What is the achievement level of our students?
    b. How can community/business leaders work with the schools to help shape success and correct problems?
    c. What programs/resources are needed to improve/assure student success? The board—in this intensified process—must make sure that the invitees to the process are an equal number of parents, community, and business leaders.

2. Schools need to open up to the community and businesses. The school district should be a source of guidance to the business and other agencies on what they could do to help students succeed. Here's how it would work:

    a. Develop a public enterprise.
    b. Modify the school curriculum to raise student awareness of businesses and civic organizations.
    c. Ensure schools are open and welcoming to the community agencies and businesses.

3. The bottom line is for a school district to put in place a two-way Linkage Process that provides a full two-way governance. When you add the Energizing/Compelling Process to the Linkage Process, the board becomes

active since it is speaking with and to the community/business/workplace leaders by asking for

a. input on what needs to happen,
b. how they should work with the schools to help students, and
c. how to correct the problems.

This, then, is the full governance that is needed to have effective schools.

THE NEXT CHAPTER

In chapter 11, we will review the material presented in earlier chapters that apply to a new governance model called the Values Governance® system. A key area is to explore student curriculum and instruction policies that unlock for the board the importance of student learning through discussion of the policy tools by the following actions:

1. Assess the existing policy.
2. Help the board determine what they want.
3. Help the board determine the policy work plan and the timeline.

The chapter then discusses implementing the Values Governance® model. The new governance model brings forward important governance elements that a Values Governance® model must contain.

More Advanced Information

As a new board member or a board member with some experience, you are not expected to read the more advanced information on the subject. However, at a later time, you can turn to chapter 21: Application-Opportunity I in the Field Manual.

Chapter 11

The New Look of the Values Governance® System in an Organization

Chapter challenge: Is there a governance system that can improve the school district governance?

Step 8: Values Governance® System

All of the materials presented in earlier chapters—chapters 4 through 10—apply to a new governance model called the Values Governance® system. The new governance model brings a greater emphasis on eight important governance elements that a Values Governance® system must contain.

We also recommend that a school board should adopt the Values Governance® system that identifies and incorporates the key values and principles of its community. An important component is to focus the school district on the importance of student learning through a discussion of its policy topic:

1. The board assesses existing policy.
2. The board determines what it wants.

The board determines its policy work that needs to be done as well as the timeline for implementation. The bottom line is engaging the customer by having public discussions that affect their children in the learning process.

KEY AREA 1—THE MAJOR JUMPING POINT

Moving to a New Governance System Called the Values Governance® System

Although there are 14,000 school systems—with an estimated 500 school districts that are using an alternative governance model—the majority of school districts across the nation need to embrace the enhanced governance model presented in the preceding chapters: the Values Governance® model. Upgrading your district governance system is your major jumping point to successfully implementing the Values Governance® system.

Implementing the Values Governance® System

Why would you decide to call the governance model a value? The definition of the word *value* is "a principle, standard, or quality considered worthwhile, or desirable."

Surely, a governance model would want to value the product of the organization: education. In chapter 8, we encouraged the board to develop a set of governance values and principles that would guide the governance of your school district. A value would also be significant to the owner or stated another way: the owner's perception of a valued product. So it is with public schools: improving student learning is the valued product and the reason that the public schools exist.

The new Values Governance® system—which concentrates on upgrading and enhancing the traditional governance school districts (see figure 11.1)—incorporates several elements that the board needs to adopt in a new governance system.

Elements of the Values Governance® Model

The *Values Governance®* model uses elements of the *traditional governance* model and adds other elements of the *alternative governance* models. Specifically, the Values Governance® model uses the Green-Line model—utilizing the *division authority role definition* with the 9:00 and 3:00 line—identifying the board domain above the line and the administrative domain below the line. In a broad perspective, this is the *role definition* of the board and the superintendent.

But the board is also responsible for the global direction of the school district. Specifically, the Values Governance® model adds the four categories found in the alternative governance models. Specifically, the Values Governance® model includes the following:

• Governance Procedure: the culture of the school district from staff treatment, officer's (CEO, CFO) roles, and so on

Figure ◀1.1. Values Governance® Model. *Source*: Copyright © 2016, Chuck Namit, Strategem LLC, Values Governance®

- Board-Superintendent-CEO Relations: the board's relationship with the superintendent that includes monitoring of CEO performance, the delegation of CEO authority, and so on
- Operational Procedure: the board's monitoring the work of the superintendent in the operational expectations of the school district, as well as human relations, budget, and financial management, and so on
- Goals: the board's direction for the school district as delineated in goals, results of student achievement, and so on

The Values Governance® model also identifies two key elements in reviewing the leadership of the school district:

- Board Self-Assessment: The board process includes the elements of the *Governance Procedure* and the *Board-Superintendent-CEO Relations*.
- Superintendent-CEO Evaluation: The board evaluates the superintendent's performance in the areas of *Operational Procedure* and meeting *Goals*.

The New Values Governance® Techniques

1. Define the roles of the board and the CEO leadership. The board governs the organization through written public policies, connecting with the

listening sessions, board meetings, and community events and with the public through organization performance. The CEO manages explicit operational expectations to meet the organization results.

2. Create a Mountain Peak of Governance by developing the Sky Bridge of Monitoring. The board creates a Mountain Peak of Governance by monitoring the organizational expectations, as well as identifying the parallel leadership of the chief governance officer (CGO) and the chief executive officer (CEO). The role of the parallel leadership (a) demonstrates the board's leadership role in policies and important decisions (b) while figuratively sending the CEO down off the mountaintop and into the valley of detail to (c) work through the operational expectations (means) of dealing with the organization's governance. Simply put, there is not a better way to explain the roles of the board and the CEO.

3. Monitor organizational expectations, throughout the year, that form the basis of the superintendent evaluation. This monitoring process stretches out the evaluative period of time, causing the board to be engaged through the year reviewing policies and monitoring the performance of the CEO. The year-long monitoring process also eliminates evaluation error of "regency of time."

4. Assure public accountability of the district leadership by employing a board self-assessment and superintendent evaluation. Using these methods—board self-assessment (How is the board doing?) and superintendent evaluation (How did he or she do?)—provides assessment and accountability to the owners and stakeholders.

5. Engage the school and community to gauge the schools. The organization and community score the schools in the fields of (a) trust, (b) relationship with the community, and (c) belief in the schools. The research of Karen L. Mapp will rate each school and place them in one of four categories: (a) Fortress School (Below-Basic School), (b) Come-If-We-Call School (Basic School), (c) Open-Door School (Proficient School), and (d) Partnership School (Advanced School).

6. Adopt a research-based curriculum and instruction program to improve student achievement. This validates the model's value that improving student learning is the primary goal of the organization: the public schools.

7. Develop a set of values principles for governance and establish a policy control status. The board develops its own beliefs, community values, and principles that define their governance for the school district. The board also formulates the basis for developing a new governance process by establishing a policy of control status to determine whether the board is a liberal, moderate, or conservative policy board. The board will be able to determine their communication and governance style while connecting more effectively with the owners of the organization.

8. Energize the community engagement process to develop a two-way governance system. These methods demonstrate a two-way governance process, as well as an ongoing method of communication between the leaders—the board and the CEO—and the owners.

The most important task for the board is to focus the board on student learning as its main duty and responsibility. The next step is for the board and CEO to establish and implement the new Values Governance® system.

The board commits to

1. Focus on student learning and policies to increase student basic achievement.
2. Achieve its goals (ends or results).
3. Communicate with its stakeholders and owners.

KEY AREA 2—ENGAGING THE BOARD IN STUDENT LEARNING POLICIES

In chapter 7, we recommended that a school district (1) examine the research of Karen L. Mapp on public school instruction and curriculum, and (2) adopt the four-stage school-community engagement model for the school district. In chapter 8, we looked at the commitment by a school district to adopt a data-based research curriculum. The bottom line, of course, is to provide the best possible curriculum for students, which is the main role of a board member.

How does Values Governance® deliver better curriculum? Developing curriculum is a core focus of the board and the school district. Surely in a school district, the key work of the school board is to unlock the need for sound student learning policy. The board also needs to focus on student learning issues that surround the policy. These issues include the following:

1. Standards: A school district establishes rigorous learning standards for students—what a student knows and the ability to perform—that will satisfy the stakeholders and owners of a public school system.
2. Assessment: A process that measures the success of students—performance and growth progress—at regular intervals.
3. Accountability: The measure of the success of a school district involves assessing students, teachers, principal, superintendent, and board at regular intervals and sharing this with the public. In chapter 8, we saw a school district measure the success of students—by data, growth, improvement, and student results—and create transparency to the stakeholders and the

owners. Accountability also includes the teacher and the principal evaluations. In chapter 6, we provided an annual assessment and evaluation system for the board and the CEO.

4. Alignment: This is how the resources—staff, standards, assessments, and funding—are used to reach the school district's goals. (In chapter 8, you can analyze a consultant firm checking a school district's horizontal and vertical alignment.)

The Values Governance® system has created a focus on student learning. The board's policy work mirrors much of what we have suggested in this book. The board should do the following:

1. Develop policy and update the policy when some work is needed (state and federal laws often impact school district work).
2. Monitor the policy and rework as needed.
3. Communicate to the public through the community engagement process.

The most important task for the board is to focus on student learning as its main duty and responsibility.

KEY AREA 3—IMPLEMENTING THE NEW VALUES GOVERNANCE® SYSTEM

The new Values Governance® system provides the board with the opportunity to take its current traditional governance model and create new Values Governance® techniques by employing the following ten elements numbers:

1. Develop a set of values principles for school governance.
2. Define the board and the CEO leadership roles.
3. Create a Mountain Peak of Governance by developing the Sky Bridge of Monitoring.
4. Monitor organizational expectations as the bases of the superintendent evaluation.
5. Assure public accountability through a board self-assessment and a superintendent evaluation.
6. Adopt a research-based curriculum and instruction program.
7. Engage the school and community to gauge their public schools.
8. Establish a communication style for the board. (Note: This can also be used by the CEO and staff.)
9. Establish a policy control status for district governance.

10. Energize community engagement to develop a two-way governance system.

Now, the board and the CEO—in their parallel leadership roles—must step forward and lead.

KEY AREA 4—TIMELINES TO IMPLEMENT A VALUES GOVERNANCE® SYSTEM

Training to implement a program requires a reasonable approach to getting stakeholders together. Training consultants can range from the school board and administrative organization's trainers to private consultant firms.

Dividing the Elements of a Values Governance® System into Logical Training Timelines

Here are the recommended training timelines to implement the Values Governance® system into the school district:

Weekend 1: Establishing School District Values, Leadership Roles, and the Monitoring Process.

1. Topics for the training:

   a. Develop a set of values principles for school governance.
   b. Define the board and the CEO leadership roles.
   c. Create a Mountain Peak of Governance by developing the Sky Bridge of Monitoring.

2. Training cadre: Consultant meets with the board, CEO, and selected cabinet/administrative staff.

   Weekend 2: Assure Public Accountability on School District Leadership.

1. Topics for the training:

   a. Monitor organizational expectations and goals as the bases of the superintendent evaluation.
   b. Utilize board self-assessment and a superintendent evaluation.

2. Training cadre: Consultant meets with the board, CEO, and selected cabinet/administrative staff.

Weekend 3: Research-based Curriculum and Gauge Public Schools.

1. Topics for the training:

   a. Adopt a research-based curriculum and instruction program.
   b. Engage the school and community to gauge their public schools.

2. Training cadre: Consultant meets with the board, CEO, and selected cabinet/administrative staff.

Weekend 4: Understanding Communication Style and Policy Control Status.

1. Topics for the training:

   a. Establish a communication style for the board and staff.
   b. Establish a policy control status for district governance.

2. Training cadre: Consultant meets with the board, CEO, and selected cabinet/administrative staff.

More Advanced Information

As a new board member or a board member with some experience, you are not expected to read the more advanced information on the subject. However, at a later time, you can turn to chapter 22: Application-Opportunity J in the Field Manual.

Part 2

GETTING THE MOST OUT OF YOUR BOARD SERVICE: A FIELD MANUAL FOR BOARD MEMBERS

This field manual portion of the book will help you develop a deeper understanding of the topics addressed earlier, in chapters 1 through 11. This advanced material provides applications and opportunities that will increase your knowledge and expertise in important subjects, which will assist you as a public servant and make you more successful and effective as a board member.

FORMAT APPROACH FOR EACH CHAPTER

Each chapter contains two parts:

Part 1: Reviewing the Essential Skills: This is a brief refresher section that relates to a corresponding chapter 1 to 11 (from the first part of the book), introducing some essential information on the subject.

Part 2: Implementing Advanced Application and Opportunity: This begins an extended discussion on the applications and opportunities for each subject—labeled as letters A through J—for most of the chapters in this second half of the book.

Purpose of a Field Manual

Helen Keller was reported to have said: "A bend in the road is not the end of the road."

So it is with board members and the superintendent that lead the school district in improving their schools. The road toward progress in governance often has "bends in the road" as they move to change the system.

In this portion of the book, we'll be focusing on board members who have been on their board for a period of time but don't see improvement in their public service or the school district. Many board members may ask: Why am I on the board? Should I run for another term?

As a consultant, I've heard many board members ask questions like these:

- How can I get better as a board member? Where can I get the training?
- My school district keeps doing the same thing. How can we improve as a school district?
- Every board member does their own thing, so how can we act together as a board?
- Why does our school district achievement—board and superintendent— seem frozen in mediocrity?
- Why aren't our graduation rates increasing in our school district?

We will explore many significant issues that board members and the district superintendent need to address to have an effective and efficient school district and maximize student learning while communicating with the owners.

Here is a preview of issues that board members must master to be an effective school board member:

- Define the role of the board and the CEO in three different governance models: the traditional governance and two alternative governance models, Policy Governance® and Coherent Governance® systems.
- Establish *values principles* for your governance system.
- Introduce *Mountain Peaks of Governance* and *Monitoring Organizational Expectations*, as well as identify the parallel leadership of the chief governance officer (CGO) and the CEO.
- Examine the accountability of board self-assessment and superintendent evaluation.
- Review the ability to gauge schools on trust, relationship, and belief in schools.
- Recommend the adoption of a research-based or data-driven curriculum.
- Establish a *communication style* and *policy control status* for the school district governance.
- Introduce techniques to *energize community engagement* in two-way governance.
- Introduce the new *Values Governance® system* model.

The field manual portion of the book is designed for more advanced information. As Peter M. Senge, author of *The Fifth Discipline* observed in a note on the book cover: "Open it up anywhere . . . cross references will lead you from defining the problem to thinking about how to solve it. Mark up the pages. Write in the margins. Draw. Scribble. Daydream."

Chapter 12

Traditional Governance System: Planning and Implementation Timelines

CHAPTER APPLICATION-OPPORTUNITY A

Part 1: Reviewing the Essential Skills

In the 1980s, the governance leadership in school districts was largely an unsettled issue. Many board members entered their office with the notion that they would *manage the school district*. The board chair or superintendent typically would contact the state school board association and request a school board trainer to work with the school district board. The goal, of course, was to avoid any conflict among well-meaning board members and the district superintendent.

Indeed, the consultants—who train school boards and superintendents—attempted to indicate that board members do not manage a school district but *govern* the school district. At the same time, trainers were in need of a model that would clarify the roles of the school board and the superintendent.

The National School Boards Association (NSBA) sought to find a model that would help school districts with their leadership. Their solution was an approach called the Green-Line Clock model. Simply put, it was a *mental model* that featured the face of a clock that would differentiate the role of the board members and the superintendent while demonstrating the school district governance process. The NSBA also wanted to help board members understand the difference between the processes of management and governance of a school district.

The NSBA approach began with an *imagineering* process that asked the board members and the superintendent to imagine that a "green line" is painted on a clock. It is a line that runs a *straight line* between the 9:00 and the 3:00 hour. Everything above the 9:00 and 3:00 hours is the *board's domain* while everything below 9:00 and 3:00 hours is the *superintendent's (administrative) domain.*

The NSBA extended the model by having the board members identify items that belong to the board in the upper part of the clock while asking the superintendents to do a similar task by citing every administrative function that is below the line.

Eventually, this became the school district leadership model for the board and the superintendent, which then became known for most of the school districts across the country as the "traditional governance" system.

Part 2: Implementing Advanced Application and Opportunity

We will discuss the traditional governance system and the training procedures for the planning and the implementation of the model. The traditional governance system emphasizes the need for clarity and coherence in the roles and responsibilities of the school board and the superintendent and school administrators.

Most governance models delineate the role of the school board as the governance team and the chief executive officer (superintendent) as the leader of the management team. Together, the *governance team* and the *management team* form the *leadership team*. The traditional governance system delineates the responsibilities of the school board and the superintendent. Training in these responsibilities—a statutory requirement in some states—includes the following:

* Policy development
* Curricular and instructional accountability
* Financial accountability
* Board-superintendent relations
* Community engagement and stakeholder linkages
* Board self-assessment and superintendent evaluation[1]

KEY AREA 1—GREEN-LINE CLOCK MODIFICATION: TRADITIONAL GOVERNANCE SYSTEM

As was mentioned earlier, the NSBA developed a clock face that examines the school board and the superintendent's work. Specifically, school board governance is shown by using the face of a clock—an old-fashioned one, not a digital clock. The traditional governance model is the most popular.

We will briefly review the elements of the "Green-Line Clock" model (see figure 12.1) and turn to procedures to implement the system.

Green-Line Clock
The Traditional Governance Model
POLICY DOMAIN

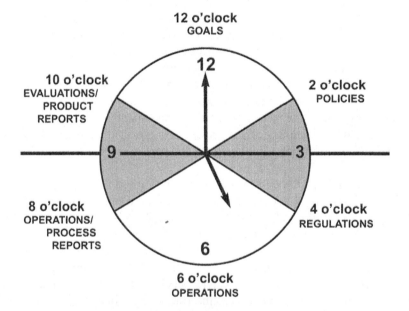

Figure 12.1.   Green-Line Clock: The Traditional Governance Model. *Source:* Copyright © 2002, David A. Steele, Professional Development Services

The points on the face of a clock represent the following:

12:00—Goals: The district-wide goals that address student outcomes. The goals are set and approved by the school board with input from the staff, community, and a planning committee.

2:00—Policies: General or global policy statements adopted by the school board to guide the professional staff in delivering the vision and goals set by the board at 12:00.

4:00—Regulations/procedures: Fine-grained means or operating expectations for achieving the 12:00 goals. Under the direction of the superintendent, the staff develops the regulations or procedures to implement policies adopted by the board. They are specifications of required action.

6:00—Operations: Actual operations of the school district: teachers teaching, custodians cleaning, bus drivers driving, principals supervising, and so on.

All the paper, e-mails, and actions at 12:00, 2:00, and 4:00 are designed to control these 6:00 operations

8:00—Monitoring operations/process reports: Reports on the 6:00 operations that tell the professional staff whether the policies and regulations are implemented as planned. Moreover, many school districts have added more monitoring reports from the superintendent to inform the school board of progress to meeting goals/results of policies. These reports tell whether the process is operating successfully. Presumably, if they are not, there will be trouble reaching the 12:00 goals.

10:00—Evaluations/product reports: Student achievement reports tell the board whether the 12:00 goals have been achieved. These reports are sometimes called the "why of education"; specifically, education reform to improve student learning. These are the most powerful measure of a school district's performance—improved student performance.

Figure 12.1 is the Green-Line Clock model. Everything that is *above* 3:00 and 9:00 is the board domain that the school board must deal with. On the other hand, everything that is *below* 9:00 and 3:00 is in the administrative domain that falls under the control of the superintendent.

The triangular areas in the clock model—above and below the 9:00 and 3:00—represent the difference in various school district governance cultures. As a long-time superintendent, David Steele observed that some school district boards go *below* the green line (the straight line that runs between 9:00 and 3:00), while some school administrators go *above* the green line. Typically, the triangle area represents areas of tension that require careful attention.[2]

Advanced Application and Opportunity: Training Sessions

The traditional governance system is tailored to meet the unique needs of school boards and school administrators. Since the material is extensive, the following training is suggested:

1. Commitment to training: The governance team and the management team must commit to attending all training sessions provided by a consultant.
2. The timing of training sessions: The training in the traditional governance model takes four weekend sessions.

   a. First weekend training session:

      —Introduction to the elements (roles and attributes) of the governance process
      —Board-superintendent relations: Developing the leadership team

b. Second weekend training session:

—Study research-based curriculum and application
—Policy review and development process

c. Third weekend training session:

—Research on school board and administrators' roles and responsibilities and integration
—Financial accountability

d. Fourth weekend training session:

—Board self-assessment and superintendent evaluation
—Community engagement and stakeholder linkages/dialogue

3. Delivery of the training: A team of consultants—with expertise and hands-on experience in the school system—will deliver the training components.
4. Follow-up training and facilitation: Trainers meet with the leadership team (governance team and management team) to review progress in implementing the governance model (e.g., six months and annual training).[3]

Chapter 13

Alternative Governance Systems: New Methods in Governance

Part 1: Reviewing the Essential Skills

As we mentioned, the simple Green-Line Clock model began the traditional governance model that divided the governance process into two domains: the board domain (area *above* the 9:00 to 3:00 line) and the superintendent or administrative domain (area *below* 9:00 to 3:00). This model worked well enough to differentiate the roles and responsibilities of the board and the superintendent. But the traditional governance model lacked the ability to precisely define the board and superintendent roles and develop the policies needed to achieve the board's goals. Something else was needed!

Scholars Develop New Governance Models

In the mid-1990s, John Carver—who developed the Policy Governance® system—completely changed the governance approach from the traditional governance model. Carver created some innovations in governance that included the following:

- Emphasized that a board should develop their governance model from their beliefs and community values
- Created, developed, and focused on thirty to forty board policies in four content categories: governance procedures, board-management relations, ends, and executive limitations (operational expectations)
- Developed a board lead calendar that contains such items as board-created policies, monitoring reports, linkage meetings, and so on, which are reviewed annually

Other scholars—Randy Quinn and Linda Dawson—developed another model called Coherent Governance®. Quinn and Dawson's model is similar to Carver's Policy Governance®. The Quinn and Dawson model allows the board to have much greater freedom to "stack out" its territory in the areas of curriculum and instruction. But from Carver's view of governance, the curriculum and instruction area is the superintendent's work as a part of executive expectation (executive limitation) and not a part of the board's work in their governance role.

At the same time, the Washington State School Directors' Association (WSSDA) consultants developed another technique that is called the concept of "parallel leadership" in school district governance and management. In effect, the chief executive officer (CEO or the superintendent) leads the administrative team while the chief board officer (CBO) leads the board team. The *administrative team* and the *board team* work together to form the *leadership team*.

All of these scholars have extended school board leadership with these innovations that challenge board members to be better governors.

Part 2: Implementing Advanced Application and Opportunity

In this Application-Opportunity chapter, we will do the following:

1. Review the alternative governance models.
2. Examine the rings of policy control.
3. Transition from a traditional governance system to an alternative governance model.
4. Determine the "Jumping-off Point: Alternative Governance Implementation Training."

KEY AREA 1—ALTERNATIVE GOVERNANCE SYSTEMS

Alternative governance models are the Policy Governance® and Coherent Governance® models. In 1997, John Carver introduced the Policy Governance® model, and Linda J. Dawson and Randy Quinn introduced the Coherent Governance® model in 2011. John Carver began the movement to an alternative governance approach from the traditional governance model, with the development of Policy Governance®. Here are some steps that are needed to define the critical elements of the Policy Governance® model.

The Theoretical Foundation of the Model: Principle Driven

The theoretical foundation of the model is principle driven. Everett Dirksen, former U.S. senator from Illinois, once observed: "My principal principle is the principle."

The Policy Governance® model is a concept of principles. Specifically, "a governing board is accountable for the organization it governs and that it exists on behalf of a larger group of persons who, either legally or (nonprofit and public organizations do not have stockholders), own the organization."[1]

John Carver's model has specific policies that define the roles and responsibilities of the CEO (superintendent) and the board, unlike the traditional governance model that's in place in most school districts. Quinn and Dawson followed suit with their similar model called Coherent Governance®. Figure 13.1 compares the four content categories for the two alternative governance models.

A Brief Review of the Four Categories of Policy

The Policy Governance® model has very few policies—between thirty and forty—and is the focus of the school board. John Carver's four categories of policies include the following:

1. Ends: The organizational "swap" with the world. What human needs are to be met, for whom, and at what cost or relative worth.

Policy Governance Model & Coherent Governance

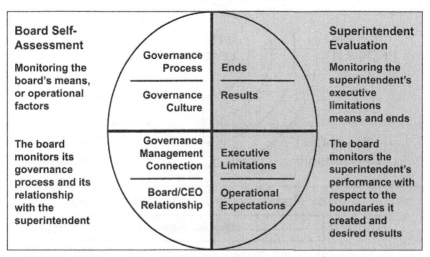

Figure 13.1. Policy Governance® and Coherent Governance®. *Source*: Copyright © 2016, Chuck Namit, Strategem LLC, Values Governance®

2. Executive Limitation: Those principles of prudence and ethics that limit the choice of staff means (practices, activities, circumstances, methods)
3. Board-Executive Relationship: The manner in which power is passed to the executive machinery and assessment of the use of the power.
4. Board Process: The manner in which the board represents the "ownership" and provides strategic leadership in the organization.[2]

Rings of Controls Determined by Reasonable Interpretation

The Any Reasonable Interpretation (ARI) marker in figure 13.2 (see arrow gauge) demonstrates a bull's-eye or targeting aspect of policies. When a board wants greater control of policies, it will add rings of policy control; therefore,

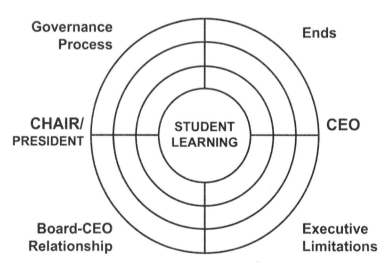

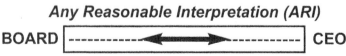

Figure 13.2.   Rings of Control Determined through Any Reasonable Interpretation by the Board. *Source*: Adapted material from John Carver & Miriam Mayhew Carver, Reinventing Your Board (Jossey-Bass Inc., 1997). Copyright © 2016, Chuck Namit, Strategem LLC, Values Governance®

the arrow gauge will move to the left. The movement of the arrow means that the board has assumed greater control over the actions of the CEO or superintendent regarding the policy. However, once the superintendent becomes adept, the board can rewrite the policies that allow more discretion for the superintendent. The arrow gauge will move to the right—fewer rings of policy control—which indicates more discretion for the superintendent in implementing the policy by use of the executive limitations or operational expectations.

KEY AREA 2—TRANSITIONING FROM TRADITIONAL GOVERNANCE TO POLICY GOVERNANCE® OR COHERENT GOVERNANCE®

When a school board decides to transition from the traditional governance model to a Policy Governance® (PG) or Coherent Governance® (CG) model, it will develop thirty to forty policies that form a new board policy manual. In effect, this forms the new school board policy manual that replaces the old policy manual. The old policy manual becomes the district policy book that the CEO or superintendent is then in charge of as the district policy and procedures book.

See figure 13.3 for information on inserting the new PG (or CG) policies on top of the district policy and procedures manual. (This original school district policy manual now becomes the CEO's responsibility.)

New PG or CG Policies Replace Current School District Policies

The original school district policy manual now becomes the CEO's responsibility.

Figure 13.3. New PG or CG Policies Replace Current Policies. *Source:* Copyright © 2016, Chuck Namit, Strategem LLC, Values Governance®

The board's role in governance is vital for successful leadership for the school district. In the alternative governance models (Policy Governance® and Coherent Governance®), the community elects the board as their representatives. The board hires a superintendent who operates the schools.

KEY AREA 3—COHERENT GOVERNANCE® IS SIMILAR TO POLICY GOVERNANCE® MODEL POLICY GOVERNANCE® RATIONALE: OBEY THE "SERVICE MARK"!

Proponents of Policy Governance® have said that consultants—particularly those who train school districts in Policy Governance®—should respect the model and the moral ownership of the idea, respect the legal control of the service mark, and maintain the purity of the model.[3] School district consultants who are the proponents of the Policy Governance® model would say that a school board member must deal with the curriculum, instructional, and other educational issues as a means (operational expectations). However, John Carver would say that these subjects (e.g., curriculum and instruction) are inappropriate in using the Policy Governance® model.

Linda Dawson and Randy Quinn work as consultants to assist clients in implementing the Policy Governance® model in school districts. The consultants, however, were aware of issues that face public education. For example, school boards must face the issues of instructional program and the quality of staff employed by the district, as well as other issues concerning such things as curriculum, assessment, accountability, and school district performance audits. Increasingly, state legislatures create new state requirements and the federal government presses the state legislators to pass laws regarding specific policies to waive requirements. Publicly elected school board members regularly must discuss and develop policies that deal with means or operating expectations and other educational issues. Put another way: the school board members must implement the state and federal laws that deal with curriculum and instruction or they will violate the law.

Coherent Governance® Elements

Although Policy Governance® and Coherent Governance® are similar models, their governance elements differ to some degree. Linda Dawson and Randy Quinn are very specific about how their four policy elements differ from John Carver's Policy Governance® model:

1. Governance Culture: All boards have a culture. In traditional governing environments, we aren't quite sure what caused it to be what it is. In

Coherent Governance®, the board deliberately and carefully crafts a set of policies that, in sum, establishes a culture for good governance.

2. Board-CEO Relations: BCR policies define the degree of authority conveyed by the board to the CEO and also outline the process for CEO evaluation.
3. Operational Expectations: Operational Expectations (OE) policies allow the board either to direct that certain conditions exist or action occurs or to prohibit those conditions and actions the board would find unacceptable. Each OE policy is clearly and unambiguously stated and has two components: one stated positively ("do this") and the other negatively ("don't do this").
4. Results: Results policies describe the outcomes that the organization is expected to achieve for the specific clients or customers it serves. "[The] results policies are the performance targets for the CEO and the organization, and form the basis for judging the success of both."[4]

KEY AREA 4—JUMPING-OFF POINT: ALTERNATIVE GOVERNANCE IMPLEMENTATION TRAINING

The alternative governance training—whether Policy Governance® or Coherent Governance®—can be implemented in four weekend sessions:

1. Weekend 1: Developing Governance Policies/Governance Culture and Policy Board Relationship/Board-CEO Relationships.
2. Weekend 2: Developing Executive Limitations/Operational Expectations.
3. Weekend 3: Developing Ends Policies/Results Policies.
4. Weekend 4: Jumping-off point from traditional governance system to the Policy Governance® and Coherent Governance®. (Note: The board and the school administration work to make the transition from one governance system to another. The board discussion with the public is an important part of the transition.)

The new board policy creates a board controlled policy system, while the previous policy guidelines are now below the district policy and procedures guidelines.

Chapter 14

Moving to a New Governance Model: Universal Principles of Governance

CHAPTER APPLICATION-OPPORTUNITY

Part 1: Reviewing the Essential Skills

Step 1: Values Governance® System

A key task of the school board is to identify the school district beliefs, community values, and principles that define their governance for the school district.

Although school boards have a similar structure (responsibilities and roles) and carry out similar functions and practices, they do not all think and act alike. The differences in school districts are due, in large part, to the differences in the constituencies they serve and the common experiences that board members may share based on school board history and community values.

The school board can learn from the authors of governance models—John Carver, Linda Dawson, and Randy Quinn—by taking its first step: the school board must be engaged in a process to examine the school district values. It is the keel that forms the basis of a locally developed governance model.

Board Discusses Beliefs, Community Values, and Principles

When a school board, along with the superintendent, decides to develop a new governance model, it must be sure that the school district beliefs and the community values represent the basis of the governance model.

In this situation, the governance planning motto applies: the difference between where we are (*current school board's governance model*) and where we want to be (*an efficient and effective governance model*) is what we do (*planning committee to develop the model*).

Though a board may have a school board history, it can develop its governance model based on values that affect the community. In preparation for this chapter, you can begin by answering the following questions:

1. What are the beliefs, principles, and values that represent our community?
2. How is governance different than management?
3. What would an effective governance system look like in our school district?

Part 2: Implementing Advanced Application and Opportunity

The goal for this chapter is a two-fold approach to develop a governance model: (1) board members identify the school district beliefs, goals, and values to develop your governance system and (2) board members review the eight Values Governance® steps that are presented in the field manual.

KEY AREA 1—VALUES PRINCIPLES FOR YOUR GOVERNANCE MODEL

One of the keys to developing a list of governance principles is to differentiate between universal and nonuniversal statements or principles that direct the board's actions in the development of a governance model. Here are some definitions that apply to developing values principles:

- *Universal principles or statements* indicate what the board wants to do or where the board wants to go in developing its goals, ends, or results for the organization.
- *Nonuniversal principles or statements* indicate how and who in the organization will do it. These nonuniversal principles are the superintendent's function and describe what he or she will do to accomplish the task.

The school board members must know the difference between a universal and a nonuniversal statement or principle. Simply put, the board directs the work of the school district through policy and employs the superintendent to specify the direction to reach the goals or results that the board prescribes.

Develop a List of Universal Principles

There is a training rule that applies in developing school board education: All school board members must be involved in school board training. Therefore, the board must engage a consultant in conducting the training.

One of the roles of a school board consultant is to assist a client—the school board and the superintendent—as they develop the school district universal principles of governance.

School board members—with the assistance of the superintendent, cabinet, and some community members—can then use this exercise to develop the school district governance model. Here are the steps the board can use:

- Board members list universal values for their school district. Other members of the committee review the list and give input.
- Once the committee develops the list, then the group reviews the list and narrows down to the agreed upon universal principles or values.
- Once there is agreement on the list, then the group begins to discuss ways that the list can be used to develop a governance model to improve the school district.

Finally, the board—with the assistance of the committee—develops a list of universal statements. The board will then review the list and check as to whether they are universal or nonuniversal statements.

KEY AREA 2—EIGHT STEPS OF THE VALUES GOVERNANCE® SYSTEM

We have presented three different forms of governance: the traditional governance and the two alternative governance models—Policy Governance® and Coherent Governance®.

Now we will present the Values Governance® system, which modifies some elements of the three governance models. It adds new elements—new concepts, tools, and practices—that give board members an enhanced view of their new governance system. This chapter, plus the rest of the book introduces the eight steps of the Values Governance® system that change and enhance the traditional governance system as follows:

Step 1: The board identifies its values and principles, developing its governing system.

Step 2: We present the Mountain Peaks of Governance and Monitoring Organizational Expectations—these provide more efficiency and consistency in governing the school district.

Step 3: The Annual Board Self-Assessment and Superintendent Evaluation processes provide a measure of assurance to the community regarding the governance of the public schools.

Step 4: The Four Phases of School-Community Engagement process allows the board to gauge the community support for its public schools.

Step 5: The school district develops a research-based curriculum that increases student learning and improves the public schools.

Step 6: Board members learn their communication style and the policy control status for governing the organization.

Step 7: The board energizes community engagement in a two-way governance approach that engages the community in the work of the school district.

Step 8: We engage the board members in a student learning discussion while pulling together all the elements of the Values Governance® system.

Chapter 15

Case Study: Monitoring Process to Resolve Issues

CHAPTER APPLICATION-OPPORTUNITY C

Part 1: Reviewing the Essential Skills

Step 2: Values Governance® System

In this chapter, we review the Mountain Peaks of Governance and Monitoring Sky Bridge of Organizational Expectations as a new method of governance. Typically, school districts use monitoring reports by the board to check the superintendent-CEO's quality of performance and adherence to a policy in dealing with school district issues. In this chapter's case study—Dallas Independent School District (DISD)—we will review the problems with the school district's budget concerns.

The board can check on the content in the ends/results policies, board-CEO relationship policies, and the executive limitations/operational expectations (means) policies through the use of monitoring reports. The Values Governance® model provides an approach that uniquely defines the roles of the board and the superintendent in governing the school district.

The Values Governance® system comes to grips with important school district issues such as budget concerns. It modifies the monitoring concept by providing a sky bridge that monitors operational expectations that provide a safe path to travel for completion of the policy or the school district issues. To provide some context for the case study, let's look at figure 15.1.

The sky bridge allows the board to cross over the bridge to reach the completed policy or issue, without having them descend into the valley of detail, which is the CEO's role or domain. Simply put, this process allows the board and CEO to remain in their appropriate domains—the board as governors

Mountain Peaks of Governance
Sky Bridge to Policy Completion

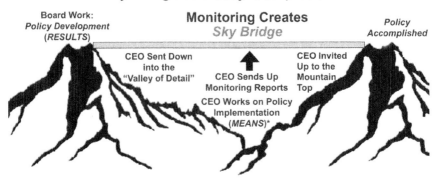

Figure 15.1.   Mountain Peaks of Governance: Sky Bridge to Policy Completion. *Source:* Copyright © 2016, Chuck Namit, Strategem LLC, Values Governance®

and the CEO as a manager of the organization's operational expectations or means.

In this chapter, we will check to see if the DISD used the Sky Bridge of Monitoring operational expectations to check on the financial condition of the district. With the Monitoring Sky Bridge of Organizational Expectations approach, there are some questions to consider as we move into implementing advanced application and opportunity: (1) Did the superintendent submit monitoring reports concerning the budget issues to the board? (2) Did the board investigate the budget crisis? (3) What avenues of action does the board possess regarding the budget crisis?

Part 2: Implementing Advanced Application and Opportunity

In this Application-Opportunity chapter, we will examine a case study of the financial condition of the DISD, as well as discuss the various "hats that consultants use" to resolve issues.

KEY AREA 1—EXPANDING THE MONITORING PROCESS

One of the most innovative processes that assists in the governance of an organization is the monitoring process—originally developed by John Carver—which incorporates monitoring the school district's culture, means (operational expectations), and ends (goals and results).

The Values Governance® system expands the potential of the monitoring process in three vital ways:

1. Focusing emphasis on the values of the board
2. Defining the specific roles of the board and superintendent
3. Providing more thorough and better governance to the staff and the community (e.g., resolving the financial difficulties of the school district)

The Values Governance® system introduces the concepts of Mountain Peaks of Governance and the Sky Bridge of Monitoring operational expectations processes that assure stakeholders and owners their organization is meeting standards of performance.

Organization's Performance

The Sky Bridge of Monitoring operational expectations process gives the board a view of the status of the CEO's performance and the organization's performance. However, in the DISD, the monitoring process was not in place. In fact, the evidence in the case study clearly shows that the board in the DISD was not monitoring the administrative work on budgetary issues of the superintendent. The result was a striking controversy with the loss of frontline teachers.

But this was one of many missteps for the school district over the years. In fact, the school district had seven superintendents in eleven years. The author—as a consultant—will indicate that this can have a dramatic impact on the climate of the school district. Moreover, the school district's staff morale would be at a low ebb.

In Key Area 2, we will review the DISD's fiscal matters that caused the school district great concern over school district operations, superintendent's performance, and school district morale.

KEY AREA 2—THE TURNING POINT: MOVING FROM A TROUBLED SCHOOL DISTRICT TO A SUCCESSFUL GOVERNANCE

External reports to a school board can be very helpful to a school district. For example, in 2008 this author wrote an article, "Dallas' Failures Can Be Remedied," for the district administration's magazine. Because this author is both a member of a school board as well as a consultant, the editors of the magazine asked the author to examine the DISD, which was dealing with a shortfall in district revenue and the consequences that would occur to the school district.

The magazine was intent upon applying the experience of a school board member and a consultant to examine the circumstances of the school district's problem. Many consultants lack any experience as a school board member. In like manner, how can the consultants know the impact that affects a school board member and school district in a crisis?

Wearing Different Hats for Different Solutions

Author Edward deBono wrote a book—*Six Thinking Hats*—based on the concept that people can wear different hats as they go through the thinking process. The genius of deBono's thought—different thinking hats for different thinking solutions—can help board members.

If you put on a different hat, you can think in a different way (e.g., a "Green Hat" means that you must think in a creative way).[1] I used deBono's idea in the case study: I wore three different thinking hats in reviewing the DISD.

Indeed, many consultants do lack the experience of serving on a school board or governance board, but consultants can look at the problem by using many thinking hats, as deBono theorized. You can see a consultant's many hats in figure 15.2 on page 119.

Dallas at a Fiscal High Noon

The DISD was examined in two ways: (1) from the external report approach in the monitoring process as well as (2) the many roles of a consultant.

As the "Ballad of High Noon" lyrics say, "Look at that big hand movin' round, nearin' high noon." Clearly, the DISD had many problems. Here are some of the problems delineated in a case study in the article, "Dallas' Failures Can Be Remedied: Sharpening a District's Leadership Model" (published in the *School Administration Magazine*, December 2008):

> The Dallas Independent School District (DISD) is $64 million in the red, with the possibility of an $84 million deficit by the end of the year. An accounting error resulted from when averaged teacher salaries were miscalculated in making budget projections. This simple error could lead to a loss of up to 3 percent of the front-line teaching staff. Moreover, the debacle appears to be the latest incident in a history of administrative missteps.
>
> The problem is more than financial. Superintendent Michael Hinojosa is the seventh superintendent in 11 years. This pattern of superintendent musical chairs must be stopped if the DISD leadership team hopes to inspire its teaching staff. Hinojosa bears the ultimate responsibility.
>
> What to do? Here are some steps that can be employed:

STEP ONE: The Policy Governance® model has two executive limitation policies—budget execution and budget planning policies—that apply to the DISD Issue. These policies require that the superintendent not "cause or allow any fiscal condition that is inconsistent with achieving the board's ends, or places the long-term financial health of the district in jeopardy." Executive limitation policies act as boundaries that rule in the superintendent's authority, as well as state the board's expectations, according to what's in place at University Place School District in Tacoma, WA.

STEP TWO: The Policy Governance® model also requires the superintendent to provide a monitoring report that must be reviewed by the board. The board, in turn, must certify the monitoring report to be either in compliance; in compliance, with stated exceptions; or not in compliance. If the board is concerned about the school district's financial condition, it can require several monitoring reports throughout the school year for the budget execution and budget planning policies.

STEP THREE: If the board has further concerns or suspicions, it can employ one of the following approaches: mandate an internal report, require an external report by a consultant, or conduct a direct inspection.

STEP FOUR: The superintendent's performance in the budget shortfall situation can be a major part of his or her evaluation. Moreover, the board can put in place a subsequent superintendent improvement plan. Improvement in this arena can be made a condition of future employment.

STEP FIVE: Finally, the goal-setting process needs to be employed through the development of superintendent or district goals regarding the financial management of the school district. The goal-setting process, of course, will create a focus for the superintendent in the coming school year.[2]

Lessons Learned from the Dallas Independent School District Experience

The DISD is similar to many school districts that have had a history of administrative missteps. So for the DISD—and many other school districts around the country—the most important fact is that the community and staff are in a constant state of disruption.

The case study shows that the DISD board faced many difficult issues: revenue concerns, finance issues, superintendent/administrative turnover, possible evaluation issues, and community and staff morale of the school system. Surely, any number of other issues can face the school board and superintendent. But chief among the issues facing a school board is the success of students and students entering our society. Indeed, essential questions were raised:

1. How can the community and staff have faith and support in a troubled school district?
2. What has the school board done to demonstrate accountability to its owners, the staff, and the students?
3. How has the school board or administration demonstrated leadership?

These three questions must be answered by the board. The consultant raised five main issues that the DISD board must address as an action plan for the future:

1. Executive Limitation Policies: Executive limitation policies act as boundaries that rule in the superintendent's authority regarding school district issues.
2. External Report as a Monitoring Report: If the board is concerned about the school district's performance, it can require several monitoring reports throughout the school year from an external source.
3. Superintendent Performance Review: The superintendent's performance can be a major part of his or her evaluation.
4. Possible Job Action: The board can require a Superintendent Improvement Plan or separation of the superintendent from the job.
5. Goal-Setting Process: The aim is to restore to the staff and the community a sense of support for the school district.

The bottom line on these five issues is that the board must delegate so that an action plan can be developed and change will take place.

Consultants Wear Many Hats

To give readers a better understanding of the many hats that a consultant can wear, we will examine the hats they wear so that you can use them in the most fruitful manner. As you will see, a consultant can view problems from many different ways or by using different hats. See figure 15.2.

Consultants typically use several techniques in dealing with complex issues and problems, as they view a problem as an external report. A consultant can be in various roles:

Trainer's Role

A trainer is one who trains and coaches clients. As a trainer, the school district miscalculation could be called "Dallas at a Fiscal High Noon." The DISD had many problems. Here are some of the problems:

1. The DISD miscalculated the average teacher salaries in the budget.
2. The district budget is $64 million in the red, with the possibility of an $84 million deficit by the end of the year.
3. This deficit could cause up to 3 percent of the teachers to be let go.

Hats Trainers/Consultants Wear

Figure 15.2. Hats Trainers/Consultants Wear. *Source*: Copyright © 2016, Chuck Namit, Strategem LLC, Values Governance®

Facilitator's Role

A facilitator is someone who makes progress to a goal easier by assistance, as a helper, or by providing support. As a facilitator, I would remind the school district of the consequences of low morale in the school district. Most of you would raise the question: What kind of morale would we have as staff if things changed (e.g., new superintendent)? Ultimately, the superintendent bore the ultimate responsibility. But, I would also add that the board had responsibility.

Consultant's Role

A consultant is one who gives an expert or professional advice to a client or organization. The author—who wrote the article as if I were the consultant—gave five recommendations, but first, the school district leadership team—the board and superintendent—must take responsibility. The DISD has five steps that it must accomplish to take charge. (Note: You can review these steps on page 118.)

A Tip of the Hat to Creative Mountain Peak Governance

We have written about the monitoring process in this Application-Opportunity chapter, but the old lesson from John Bytheway still applies: "Inch by inch things are a cinch, but yard by yard, it gets hard."

By employing the "inch-by-inch" concept of Mountain Peaks of Governance and the Sky Bridge of Monitoring operational expectations, you can better serve the owners—the community—with better governance.

Chapter 16

Applications of Board Self-Assessment and Superintendent Evaluation

CHAPTER APPLICATION-OPPORTUNITY D

Part 1: Reviewing the Essential Skills

Step 3: Values Governance® System

Through the self-assessment and the evaluation processes, goals are revised and improved, which facilitates the work of the school district. Before putting an evaluation process in place, the board must answer these questions:

1. How well has the board performed as the governor of the school district?
2. What are the ethical and legal requirements of the superintendent?
3. What are the purposes and goals of the evaluation?[1]

KEY AREA 1—TIMING OF THE INTEGRATED BOARD SELF-ASSESSMENT AND SUPERINTENDENT EVALUATION PROCESSES

Steps for the school board and superintendent leadership to incorporate the integrated process follow a school district calendar. Whenever the board hires a new superintendent or the current superintendent is under a contract for future employment, the board self-assessment and the superintendent evaluation cycles begin on or about July 1. For example, let's assume that the board is hiring a new superintendent. The following steps apply:

1. Selecting the superintendent: Many school districts hire a consultant who develops a process to search for candidates and works with the community

to get input from the school district stakeholders. Typically the search for a new superintendent begins in January.

2. Developing a superintendent evaluation instrument: In preparation for the hiring of a superintendent, the board should review the current evaluation form and procedure. Once you hire the superintendent, the instrument should be reviewed by your hire and asked whether there are recommendations for change.
3. Formalizing an evaluation process, including the procedures and the timing: School boards evaluate the performance of the superintendent on more than one occasion. For example, the superintendent has an interim evaluation in January or February, and a final summative evaluation concludes the year in June or July.
4. Board directing the CEO to review the strategic plan or strategic framework: The CEO, in successive steps, reviews the school district's strategic plan or strategic framework. The review of the strategic plan or strategic framework is then reported back to the board by the superintendent.
5. Establishing goals for the superintendent: The development of goals for the superintendent should come from at least three sources: Global-Level Goals (strategic framework or strategic plans), Board-Related-Level Goals (board self-assessment), and Superintendent-District-Level Goals (long-range goals that take multiple years to complete).
6. Defining the limits of the superintendent's authority: In a Values Governance® system, policy lays out the authority that a superintendent can rely on. The superintendent's authority—budget authority and other parameters—are laid out in a similar fashion in policy.
7. Monitoring the superintendent's implementation of policies: Monitoring of the superintendent's implementation of policies sharpens the performance and is endorsed by the Values Governance® system. The monitoring procedure requires the superintendent to report on the implementation of the policies.[2]

Between November and January, the board conducts a midyear evaluation of the superintendent, which gives the superintendent a chance to apprise the board on progress to meeting goals that were established for him or her at the beginning of the school year in July. The meeting of goals also provides the superintendent with the opportunity to discuss the goals because of circumstances that affect these goals.

In March or April, the school board undertakes a board self-assessment of itself. The board's goal in its self-assessment is to examine its governance process and practices, as well as to review the board-superintendent relationship. Another part of the self-assessment process is to review the progress to achieving the district's goals for the current year and plan for next year's goals. In summary, the board is asking an important question: how well is the board doing?

The board self-assessment and superintendent evaluation process (see figure 16.1) clearly shows that the circle at the top of the model demonstrates the traditional governance model division of the board's domain, while the administration or superintendent's domain is on the bottom as demonstrated in chapter one (see figure 1.1 on page 7). This model also applies to the alternative governance systems regarding the roles and the responsibilities of the board and the superintendent. The Values Governance® system

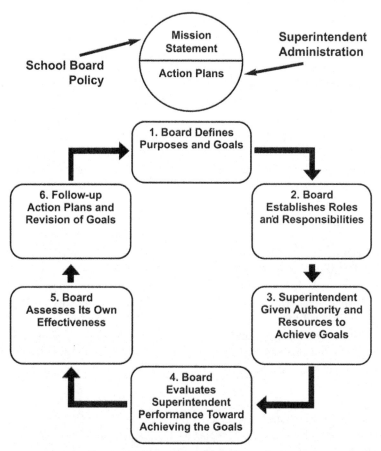

Figure 16.1.   Board Self-Assessment and Superintendent Evaluation. *Source:* Copyright © 2016, Chuck Namit, Strategem LLC, Values Governance®

emphasizes that the material in figure 16.1 applies equally to all governance systems.

There is an old business school adage that applies to governance: Never allow your boss to be surprised. Here, the "boss" is the school board that employs the superintendent.

Note: The Board Self-Assessment and Superintendent Evaluation (figure 16.1) processes have been adapted from an approach used by the Iowa School Board Association material to illustrate the energizing principles of Values Governance®.

KEY AREA 2—DEVELOPING THE SUPERINTENDENT EVALUATION INSTRUMENT

The Values Governance® evaluation instrument helps the board do its work in evaluating the CEO or superintendent. The evaluation instrument must contain the following:

1. The board defines purpose and goals: The Values Governance® system has a policy that details the board's expectation of the superintendent.
2. The board establishes roles and responsibilities: The Values Governance® system is very specific about defining the board's role (results or goals) and the CEO or superintendent's roles (operational expectations).
3. The board defines the superintendent's delegated authority and resources: Ends or results are the goals that are defined in board policies.
4. The board assesses its own effectiveness: Another term to describe this action is the board self-assessment. The board examines its role and practices, develops goals, and defines its expectations for the superintendent to perform.[3]
5. The board evaluates superintendent performance in light of progress to a goal. In the Values Governance® system, the board does an interim evaluation of the superintendent between November and January, with a final evaluation in June.
6. Follow-up action plan and revision of goals in light of progress: This is a two-fold process: (a) set or refine a goal or result and (b) establish the district's contractual relationship with the superintendent in May or June.[4]

Salary discussions and contractual obligations with the CEO or superintendent can be, and frequently are, a part of this discussion. This author suggests that the board first discuss contractual issues with legal counsel.

KEY AREA 3—ELEMENTS OF SUPERINTENDENT
EVALUATION INSTRUMENTS[5]

The superintendent, as CEO, serves as the educational leader of the district and must implement the board policies. The following areas evaluate the performance of the superintendent:

1. Board/Superintendent Relations Communication
2. Strategic Management/Direction of the District
3. Operational Leadership of the District
4. Facilities Management, Personnel, and Staff Relations
5. Implementation of Policy
6. Financial Leadership of the District
7. External and Community Relations
8. Professional Growth

In effect, these are the skills that a CEO or superintendent uses in reaching the operating expectations or means. Each of the categories has a set of five descriptive indicators, which are rated on the following scale:

1. Unsatisfactory
2. Needs Improvement
3. Satisfactory
4. Good
5. Excellent

The Values Governance® system has added a separate section for evaluating the superintendent's goals or results of the school district by examining the school district goals that are established by the board and superintendent. These school district goals might include such things as Math, Science, Reading, Language Arts, Student Support (Engagement and Discipline), Community Engagement, and Operational and Fiscal Effectiveness.

You can rate each school district goal on a number scale that ranges from 1 (poor) up to 10 (excellent). Consequently, the total of the Descriptive Indicators' Score of the Superintendent and the School District Goals' Score will form the final score, which is the Total Score for the Superintendent Evaluation.[6]

In summary, the Values Governance® system provides an integrated method for the board to self-assess, while evaluating the superintendent. Moreover, the statutes in some states require the evaluation of the superintendent.

KEY AREA 4—VALUES GOVERNANCE® SYSTEM: BOARD SELF-ASSESSMENT INSTRUMENT

Here is a list of elements that could be in a Values Governance® Board Self-Assessment Instrument. A board can use the list as a discussion item when they develop their instrument.

1. Board-superintendent relations: Develops and maintains a relationship with the superintendent.
2. Board meeting effectiveness and efficiency: Encourages initiatives to improve the conduct and productivity of the school board meeting.
3. Board-community relations: Supports open dialogue with the community and local and state governmental leaders.
4. Board qualities: Includes knowledge, independence, and respect for one another and decisions by the full board.
5. Personnel relations: Provides appropriate staffing for the needs of the school system.
6. Board instructional programs relations: Provides oversight to revise, update, and monitor the instructional programs to improve student learning.
7. Financial management monitoring: Provides oversight for the district's financial condition.
8. Policy development: Develops timely and appropriate policies to govern the school district.
9. Goal setting and planning: Plans, develops, and implements appropriate goals.
10. Media relations: Develops effective strategies for communicating via media.
11. Leadership and school district culture: Develops a professional learning community through continuous improvement, team identity, and high expectations.
12. Policy implementation and governance as part of the leadership team: Implements board policies while dealing with means issues.
13. Communication and community relations: Proactively engages and learns the community's expectations for the public schools.
14. Financial management: The board is the steward of the district's finances.
15. Values and ethical leadership: Demonstrates ethical behavior in leading the school district.
16. District goals: Evaluates and implements the global, board, and district operational goals.[7]
17. Building legislative relations: Builds working relationships with local legislators and other locally elected officials.

KEY AREA 5—THE CONTRACTUAL RELATION
WITH THE DISTRICT

The evaluation process reviews the superintendent's progress to meeting the current district goals (ends, results) for the next school year.

A final step then comes into play: the superintendent's performance review or evaluation forms the basis of his or her contractual status. The board can also seek the advice of the school district's legal counsel regarding the contractual relations with the superintendent.

KEY AREA 6—DEVELOPING GOALS, ENDS,
AND RESULTS

Assessment and evaluation are the ultimate accountability and development of goals, ends, or results to improve the product. For education, that product for the owners (community or stakeholders) is improving student learning.

The three major governance models that we have spoken about have different ways of discussing goals. For the Values Governance® system, the board's major job is to shape the district's goals from three sources: global, board, and district-level goals.

Three-Tiered Approach: Goal (Ends or Results) Development

An important part of every board is to develop goals for the organization. Goal development is especially true for the Values Governance® system.

The three-tiered approach for goal development is a process that can be used to assist the board in developing the goals (ends or results).

The governance of a school district can assist in the distinction of various goal levels. The board's governance process and board-CEO relations' topics are the basis of board self-assessment goals, whereas operational expectations and goals' topics are the basis for superintendent evaluation goals.

Global-Level Goals (Ends, Results)

These are district goals (flowing from the superintendent evaluation process) and strategic planning goals that are more global in nature. The school district accomplishes these goals over several years.

Here is an example: create an effective schools' research-based plan of work focusing on a clearly aligned, articulated, comprehensive instructional program that has as its intended result the improvement of student achievement.

Procedures: operational expectations for the CEO:

1. Develop and implement a comprehensive and sustainable professional development program based on the "Effective Schools' Plan of Work" for teachers, administrators, and paraprofessionals.
2. Develop a process with timelines for the implementation of the changes to the school district's grade level configuration.

Board-Level Goals (Ends, Results)

These are goals (ends, results) that flow from the board self-assessment process.

Here is an example: Ensure that there is a consistent customer service attitude that promotes respect across the district.

Procedures: operational expectations for the CEO:

1. Coordinate with the director of community relations, the continued implementation of the district's "Communication Plan of Work."
2. Work with appropriate constituencies to assure continued district fiscal stability while simultaneously addressing long-term technology needs.

District-Level Goals (Ends, Results)

These are superintendent operational goals (ends, results). Often, these goals flow from the global-level goals that have an annual benchmark that must be met to accomplish the long-term goals.

Here is an example: create a comprehensive and sustainable K–12 continuum of interventions for meeting students' academic and other special needs to include special education, ELL, and at-risk/alternative students.

Procedures: operational expectations for the CEO:

1. Implement a comprehensive "K–12 Mathematics Plan" that includes the successful implementation of the new curriculum for the middle schools and high school levels during the 20xx–20xx school year.
2. Develop a comprehensive "K–12 Science Plan" that includes the successful implementation of new science curriculum at the high school level during the 20xx–20xx school year.
3. Develop and present for school board approval by March 20, 20xx, school district boundary revisions for the 20xx–20xx and 20xx–20xx school years.
4. Work with appropriate personnel to assure the successful completion (on time and within budget) of district capital projects.

Table 16.1. Goals, Ends, Results: Operational Expectations

Goals, Ends, Results	Operational Expectations
Board Work	Board Work for CEO
1. Develop	To implement a comprehensive
2. Create	Process with timelines. . .
3. Develop	Sustainable work plan. . .
4. Vision	Present. . .
5. Ensure	Consistent . . . Coordinate. . .

Source: Copyright © 2016, Chuck Namit, Strategem LLC, Values Governance®

SETTING GOALS, ENDS, AND RESULTS

To provide you with some practice in the setting of goals, ends, and results, here is a study exercise that will get the practice needed to be successful.

Take-the-Wheel Exercise: Action Words and Phrases

Certain action-oriented words and phrases jump-start your goals while motivating the board, superintendent, and staff to implement the goals (see table 16.1). Following are some examples.

Global-Level Goals (Ends, Results)

These are district goals (flowing from the superintendent evaluation process) and strategic planning goals that are more global in nature. The school district accomplishes these goals over several years.

Plug in your goals, ends, or results: "_____."

    Procedures: operational expectations for the CEO:

1.
2.

Board-Level Goals (Ends, Results)

These are goals that flow from the board self-assessment process.
Plug in your goals, ends, or results: "_____."
Procedures: operational expectations for the CEO:

1.
2.

District-Level Goals (Ends, Results)

These are superintendent operational goals. Often, these goals flow from the global-level goals that have an annual benchmark that must be met to accomplish the long-term goals.

Plug in your goals, ends or results: "_____."
Procedures: operational expectations for the CEO:

1.
2.

KEY AREA 7—KEY TO GOVERNANCE SUCCESS AGENDA: SUPERINTENDENT EVALUATION AND BOARD SELF-ASSESSMENT PROCESS

To get the board to work on next year's goals, ends, or results, a training exercise has been included on a Key to Governance Agenda. A consultant or trainer can assist the board in discussing the topics. Here is a sample agendum that can be used with the school board and CEO to develop the training.

Key to Governance Agenda

1. Purpose: Accountability to the Public: Assessment and Evaluation Process
2. Governance Structure of Public Schools (Values Governance®, traditional governance, Policy Governance®, and Coherent Governance® systems)
3. Board Self-Assessment and Superintendent Evaluation Processes
4. Board Self-Assessment Process and Samples
5. Board Self-Assessment Exercises: Plug-and-Chug Work Session
6. Superintendent Evaluation Process and Samples
7. Superintendent Evaluation Samples
8. Superintendent Evaluation Exercises: Plug-and-Chug Work Session
9. Succession Planning Process
10. Succession Planning Exercises: Plug-and-Chug Work Session
11. Review the Three-Tiered Goal-Setting Process (global-, board-, and district-level goals)
12. Superintendent Contract Process (final superintendent evaluation and contract considerations)
13. Sample Superintendent Contract

KEY AREA 8—THE RESULTS OF BOARD TRAINING

Training for advanced or beginning board members can be very fruitful for board leadership and the school district. Here is a response from a new board member, following the training:

"The processes of board self-assessment and superintendent evaluation allow the board and the superintendent to stop and take a moment to ensure that everyone is on the same page and working in the same direction," says Kathryn Lerner, board member of the Snoqualmie School District, Washington. "Is this still the best plan for kids? Do we need to revisit our priorities based on changes in funding, student needs, and community preferences? Is this the best way to spend our money? The tools should be directly tied to the district's mission, vision, and goals," she adds. "By taking the time to have this conversation and do this work, school board members, and the superintendent can ensure that they are working in concert with one another on behalf of the students and taxpayers of their community."[8]

Ultimately, a superintendent added the final note that signaled when the board self-assessment and the superintendent evaluation worked for better governance: "Integrating a superintendent evaluation process with a school board self-assessment has helped build a stronger team," said Rick Schulte, former superintendent, Oak Harbor School District, Washington.[9]

What We've Learned in the Application-Opportunity

Theme: Evaluation and assessment of the organization's officer provides accountability to stakeholders and owners.

1. In the Values Governance® system, the assessment and evaluation processes are essential to improving the governance of the organization.
2. The assessment process is gathering information about the organization or school district performance as it relates to the governance process. The school district represents the stakeholders and owners. It answers the question, "How is it going?" In the board self-assessment process, we ask, "How well is the board doing?" The board—in a self-assessment process—attempts to measure its purpose, roles, responsibilities, goals, and ultimately its performance.
3. Superintendent evaluation comes to the board in a summative evaluation package. The board reviews the goals and operational expectations, which then creates a discussion of the CEO's performance during the year. The elements of the evaluation instrument looks at the several factors:

   • The strengths and weaknesses of the superintendent, which typically leads to board-CEO dialogue

- Needed dialogue pertaining to the CEO's performance regarding the board's goals and objectives for the school district
- Use of the three-tiered approach to develop board goals for the coming year
- A review of the general state of the organization from many vantage points
- The board's expectation of the organization (owners)
- A review of the contractual obligations with the superintendent

4. Typically, a consultant will present a training program to the board and superintendent that assists the parties in board self-assessment and superintendent evaluation.

Chapter 17

Checking and Charting Your School and Community Stages

Part 1: Reviewing the Essential Skills

Step 4: Values Governance® System

The Values Governance® system encourages each school district to employ Karen L. Mapp's research in reviewing the status of each school in your district. In this Application-Opportunity chapter, we provide a complete system of checking and charting your school community stage for your school building.

Mapp, a Harvard professor, shared her latest research on the four school-community engagement stages at a state association meeting. Mapp presented her research to school board members at a conference. At the same time, the author sat at a table and drew a four-square window diagram that placed Mapp's findings in each of the four windows. This approach was shared with Mapp at the end of the presentation, in which she expressed some interest.

Values Governance® encourages the use of the four-square model—embedded with Mapp's research—to demonstrate the four school-community engagement stages.[1]

Let's Examine the School-Community Engagement Model

The reader should examine the School-Community Engagement model (table 17.1), which is a quadrant, with the upper part of the model describing the four stages of school development, based on Mapp's research.

133

Part 2: Implementing Advanced Application and Opportunity

Key Area 1—Four Stages of Schools in Mapp's Research

Mapp's research identified four levels of schools that distinguish the school success and attitude to the stakeholders and owners:

Stage 1: Fortress School (Below-Basic): The school is combative to the owners and stakeholders, with low trust, relationship, and belief in their schools.

Stage 2: Come-If-We-Call School (Basic): The school views itself as in containment to the owners and stakeholders, with a low-to-moderate trust, relationship, and belief in their schools.

Stage 3: Open-Door School (Proficient): The school seeks accommodation with the owners and stakeholders, with moderate trust, relationship, and belief in their schools.

Stage 4: Partnership School (Advanced): The school sees itself in collaboration with the owners and stakeholders, with high trust, relationship, and belief in their schools.[2]

School district administrators need to meet with stakeholders and owners to chart the performance of the schools within the district and apply Mapp's four-stage model.

KEY AREA 2—TAKE-THE-WHEEL EXERCISE: GAUGE YOUR SCHOOLS

A school board will undoubtedly want to examine the schools in its school district and determine where each school belongs in the four school-community engagement stages. In chapter 8, we present the North Thurston Public Schools, Washington, as a representative case study because it had decided to implement a data-driven curriculum.[3] As we go through this exercise, we will reference its experiences.

Numbers Count in Analyzing a School

You can apply the four school-community engagement stages in several ways. For example, in a smaller school district—with one or more elementary schools, a middle school, and a high school—the study can be done independently with each school doing its analysis. In a larger school district, a school district may be divided into school zones. Each school zone covers a region—with various elementary schools, middle schools, and a high school or two—that a school district uses in its governance and management of the school district.

Whether the school district is in a small school district—with few schools—or in a larger school district—with many schools and zones—the district will have to come to conclusions on schools; therefore, the board must set a direction for the district through its policy and develop operating expectations for the superintendent.

Schools Can Be Effective in Performance

Participants in the exercise must understand that to change a school's performance, you must adopt principles of effectiveness, such as the following five examples:

1. Creating a vision: High-performance school districts create a vision for the type of schools and district they seek.
2. The academic program: Choosing the content of the academic program is fundamental to the quality of the graduate's education and, thereby, the quality of the district.
3. The accountability component: Student progress must be monitored in time to permit teachers to adjust instructional content and methodology.
4. Managing teaching and learning: A formal management process to monitor teaching and learning across the entire district and for each building is essential.
5. Developing system capacity: Investments in the capacity of teachers and administrators to design, implement, and manage this system will produce welcome returns.

Take-the-Wheel Exercise: Broad Participation Is Vital to Analyzing a School Community Stage

The "take-the-wheel exercise" is an activity that allows the board, administration, customers, and owners to take part in gauging the level of trust in all schools of the district. This is part of the Values Governance® linkage, dialogue, and community engagement techniques that we have proposed throughout this book. Common elements include the following:

1. Engage key community, business, and workplace leaders, stakeholders, and owners, thereby reaching out to these groups to assist with the first

step in the process. The participation must also be broad in engaging a variety of people, such as the following:

- Staff: teachers, paraprofessionals, bus drivers
- Principal
- Local elected officials
- News media
- Business leaders
- Community leaders
- Target stakeholders
- Owners
- Civic groups
- Clients
- Parents

2. Create a common agendum: The difference between the current situation and gaining a common vision is gaining a consensus on what needs to happen. The school district needs to communicate with such groups as the key community, business, and workplace leaders, as well as stakeholders and owners.
3. Map the children's location in your district: A school district can map the location of special needs families and students in the school district.
4. Identify the needs and helping resources within the community: The board, administration, and community/business/workplace leaders engage in the process of identifying the needs and resources needed to help students.
5. Review the four stages of school-community schools: This aspect of the model can be political—no school principal, staff, or other employees would like to be identified at stages 1 or 2. Therefore, the customers and the owners want each school of the district to be identified at stages 3 or 4. To accomplish this task, the customers and owners need to be able to rely on the quality of their schools.

To review what was stated earlier, let's look again at the four stages of schools that come from the research of Karen L. Mapp.

Stage 1: Fortress School (Below-Basic): The school is combative to the owners and stakeholders.
Stage 2: Come-If-We-Call School (Basic): The school views itself as in containment to the owners and stakeholders.
Stage 3: Open-Door School (Proficient): The school seeks accommodation with the owners and stakeholders.
Stage 4: Partnership School (Advanced): The school sees itself in collaboration with the owners and stakeholders.[4]

Checking and Charting Your School-Community
Stage for Your Building

Competency: It is important to develop a trust relationship with the staff. Gauging the level of trust permits you to identify the development stage and also gives the staff the ability to participate in improving student learning.

Staff members need to consider the questions concerning their role in improving student learning. See table 17.1 on page 137.

1. From your vantage point (stakeholder, owner, staff, principal, etc.), at what stage is your current relationship with the following group(s) or person(s)? Note: Place a "C" for the current stage of the relationship by the appropriate group(s) or person(s) in table 17.1.
2. One year from today, what stage would you see your future relationship with the group(s) or person(s) listed? Note: Place an "F" for the future stage of the relationship by the appropriate group(s) or person(s) in table 17.1.
3. The bottom line in designating a "C" for current stage and an "F" for the future stage in the following year is as a school district you are attempting to reach consensus for changes to improve student learning.

Table 17.1.   Checking and Charting Your School Community Stage*

Member/Group	Stage 1: Fortress School (Below Basic)	Stage 2: Come-If-We Call (Basic)	Stage 3: Open-Door School (Proficient)	Stage 4: Partnership (Advanced)
1. Staff				
2. Principal				
3. Local Elected Officials				
4. Media				
5. Business Leader				
6. Community Leader				
7. Stakeholder				
8. Owners				
9. Civic groups				
10. Clients				
11. Parents				

* Note: The four stages of schools above come from the research of Karen L. Mapp.

Source: Adapted from the research of Karen L. Mapp, *Moving Forward: Building the Capacity for Effective Family Engagement*, 2012. Copyright © 2016, Chuck Namit, Strategem LLC, Values Governance®

4. Closing the gap between your current school stage and future school stage of the relationship is your goal. Make your goal as specific as possible. State the appropriate elements of the goals for numbers 1 through 5.

(1) Our staff relationship goal is:

_____
_____
_____
_____
_____

(2) Problems or blockages that prevent attainment of the goal:

_____
_____
_____
_____
_____

(3) Strengths that your team can build on to attain the goal:

_____
_____
_____
_____
_____

(4) Internal and external resources to assist in the attainment of the goal (e.g., local, state, or federal resources, training opportunities):

_____
_____
_____
_____
_____

(5) Action plans for attainment of the goal (e.g., each strategy/task must be specific, measurable, time-related, and attainable):

_____
_____
_____
_____
_____

This process allows community leaders to emerge. This new leadership becomes the basis of a helping community outreach to attain student learning improvement.

What We've Learned in the Application-Opportunity

Theme: A board must understand the four school-community engagement stages, chart and rank each school, and how it will support its stakeholders and owners.

1. The board will undoubtedly want to use Mapp's research (the four stages of schools as listed in the chapter) to examine each of its schools to see which stage the school is placed.

2. This review by the school district gives the stakeholders and owners an opportunity to use the take-the-wheel exercise to determine where each of its schools see themselves. Using Karen L. Mapp's research, each school can be examined so that key communicators can gauge the current school stage with a "C" place in the stage and then, after a year-long planning phase, an "F" is designated for the future stage. The take-the-wheel exercise can be used as you implement the linkage, dialogue, and community engagement approaches that are used to improve student learning.

Chapter 18

Case Study: Leadership Implementing a Research-Based Curriculum

Part 1: Reviewing the Essential Skills

Step 5: Values Governance® System

The development of an innovative curriculum for the school district students is a vital factor in their success. The Values Governance® system believes the board should adopt a research-based or data-driven curriculum to achieve this success.

In this Application-Opportunity chapter, we provide an extensive case study on the North Thurston Public Schools Board adoption of an effective schools' research-based curriculum.

Part 2: Implementing Advanced Application and Opportunity

This case study has three key areas: Key Area 1 is a quick review of the steps that are needed to implement a research-based curriculum; Key Area 2 will review the implementation of a strategic framework that improves student learning, develops financial stability for the school district, and develops a new culture of compassion for the school district and the community; and Key Area 3 deals with other management changes and the constancy of leadership change.

Specifically, Key Areas 1 and 2 of this case study come from internal documents of the North Thurston Public Schools on an Effective Schools model and the implementation of a strategic framework that improves student learning.

For a school board and the district administration, implementing this case study material will accomplish two things: (1) provide the steps to develop an innovative school curriculum to improve student learning and (2) develop a strategic framework to implement the curriculum and fully engage the community.

This application-opportunity case study will examine the steps needed to provide the data needed to measure student progress and increase student achievement.

The case study will also deal with the reform issues that a school district must address:

1. Put school reform and innovation into action.
2. Develop financial stability for a school district.
3. Change a school district and community culture.
4. Review the various education initiatives that occur in the state and national scene.
5. Develop strategic framework and leadership change.

KEY AREA 1—CREATING A CHANGE PROCESS: IMPLEMENTING A RESEARCH-BASED CURRICULUM

A school board and administration—to face the public challenge of the relevance of the school district curriculum—must ask themselves the question: How can the school district ensure that the children are getting the best possible education? This question is one that is vital to a board member's service: securing the best possible curriculum for the students.

In their book, *Good Governance Is a Choice*, Linda Dawson and Randy Quinn raise the issue of "confused accountability." Is that a decision of the school board or the superintendent? To answer this question, Dawson and Quinn simply use a statement: "The simple rule is the party who makes the decision should be held accountable for the results of the decision."[1]

Here are four steps for the implementation of a research-based curriculum:

Step 1: Board Initiative to Search for a Research-Based Curriculum

The North Thurston Public Schools Board asked for the administration to review the research-based curriculum models and bring a recommended model back to the board for consideration. Specifically, the board then directed the superintendent to explore consultant firms who could do the following:

1. Audit the entirety of each school in the district.
2. Point out the strengths and weaknesses of the system.
3. Make recommendations and provide training.

Based upon the administration's work, the firm—24/7 Consultants—was recommended as the consultant company to perform the school audit. The board passed a recommendation to hire the firm to do a complete horizontal and vertical audit of all schools, pointing out the strengths and weaknesses of each school, administration, and staff.

Step 2: Firm's Audit of the North Thurston Public Schools

The actual report from the 24/7 consultants is a complete horizontal and vertical audit of all schools, pointing out the strengths and weaknesses of each school, administration, and staff of the North Thurston Public Schools (NTPS). What follows is an extract section of the report on NTPS:

Case Study: 24/7 Consultants' Firm Audit

North Thurston Public School (Lacey, WA) implemented the Effective Schools Assessment method with the dates of Program Review: September—October 2004.

The Learning 24/7 Consultants were Dr. Hal Guthrie, Dr. Ray Garcia, and Robert Skaife, with supporting consultants: Laticia F. Diaz, Special Education, John Booth, Mathematics.

A summary of the audit includes the following sections:

Section 1: Overview of the Review Process

In September 2004, an on-site assessment of school and district effectiveness was conducted by Learning 24/7-NSCI in the North Thurston Public Schools. The purpose of the study was to gather data in each school and at the district level to determine the current conditions to move toward comprehensive school improvement. Specifically, the purpose was to analyze the data and recommend a comprehensive school improvement model embedded in the Effective Schools research and correlated with the State of Washington's Eight Stages of School Improvement Planning. The model presented is the Effective Schools Performance Model and referenced as the model throughout this report.

Section 2: The Effective Schools Performance Model

The recommended Effective Schools Performance Model is presented in five (5) stages. Each stage is essential and is mutually interdependent with other stages. The model is presented to outline a strategic roadmap for system-wide and individual school improvement. This model is aligned with the Eight-Step School Improvement Process adopted by the State of Washington and is correlated with the seven components of the effective school's research.

Stage 1: Creating a Vision

High-performance school districts create a vision for the type of schools and district they seek and the competencies they expect in their students.

Stage 2: The Academic Program

Choosing the content of the academic program is fundamental to the quality of the graduate's education and, thereby, the quality of the district. In an era of high-stakes accountability, where all states have adopted content standards for subjects and grade levels, the place to start is with the State of Washington's current Standards and Grade Level Expectations.

Stage 3: The Accountability Component

Benchmark assessments are incremental snapshots of student performance data taken periodically throughout the course of instruction. Student progress must be monitored in time to permit teachers to adjust instructional content and methodology. All academic performance issues must be identified and remediated before the conclusion of the year, course, or state assessment cycle.

Stage 4: Managing Teaching and Learning

A formal management process to monitor teaching and learning across the entire district and for each building is essential. System-wide academic performance is analyzed and prioritized into three to five annual improvement goals. A summary of all available performance data enables the board, superintendent, and instructional personnel to identify and manage the district's instructional focus.

Stage 5: Developing System Capacity

Investments in the capacity of teachers and administrators to design, implement, and manage this system will produce welcome returns. High-performance systems have a clear focus and a clearly articulated plan.

Summary

The Learning 24/7 team is honored to be chosen for this important work in the North Thurston Public Schools. Every state in the nation has developed standards and expectations for K–12 students academic performance. Accountability systems accompany these academic expectations, requiring most schools and districts to undertake systemic change. We are pleased to provide this service to North Thurston in this important journey and commend its vision to take these steps.[2]

Step 3: The Olympian Editorial of 24/7 Audit

The Olympian newspaper wrote an editorial regarding the 24/7 Consultant firm audit report of the North Thurston Public Schools. This report had a tremendous impact on the community, which demonstrated the school district was a leader in the field of education reform. On December 4, 2004, the Olympian published an editorial quoting Jim Koval, the superintendent:

> All of our schools, along with district administration, will be performance-audited. This will include a close look at every office, every classroom, every school community, to see whether we're all doing the things we need to do to make the progress we need to make. In other words, we want to know whether we're all rowing in the same direction—and using the right oars!

And so began the introduction of a science-based curriculum in the North Thurston Public Schools. As the newspaper chronicled in the editorial:

> The third-party audit, performed by a Phoenix-based review company, was the first step in a five-year process to adopt the national 'Effective Schools'

research model. The goal is to create a system that will provide an equitable educational experience for all students. . . . Students, parents, teachers, administrators and taxpayers are well served by that attitude favoring openness and independent review.

Other observations by the 24/7 consulting firm:

The audit noted many strengths in the 19-school district: a history of rising test scores, a strong level of community involvement and an assortment of teaching strategies. Areas where improvements are suggested: making sure textbooks and class materials are closely tied to the state's learning standards, more frequent student assessments, and working to identify and then help struggling students early on.

Koval said, "There were no huge surprises in the 92-page report by Learning 24/7. But, the Phoenix-based firm gave district administrators clear recommendations to follow. We've tried a lot of good things in the past several years, but I think there is a tendency to try everything, and sometimes that's not the best approach to getting better. Sometimes things stick to the wall, and sometimes they don't."

The audit gives North Thurston clear direction on what is working and what is not. The next step is to make the systemic changes recommended in the audit. That's not an easy task, but it's one the district must pursue. Administrators must put a plan together that will—to use Koval's analogy—keep all the partners in the North Thurston District rowing in the same direction.

The true gauge of success will be measured in the academic progress of individual students.

In summary, the board—in a governance sense—had accepted the responsibility/accountability for establishing a research-based curriculum, with the board's action of passing the recommendation and delegating to the superintendent—and his staff—to continue with developing more successful students. Historically, this was the board's first step in becoming fully accountable to the community. It was also the beginning of a very long process of the school district to improve its schools.

Upon the conclusion of the research-based curriculum audit, the board delegated to the superintendent to begin—with school district staff—to employ techniques that would assist the district's teachers in reaching out to students to improve their performance.

Step 4: Train Administrators, Teachers, and the Union to Support the New Research Curriculum

The board took the next steps. The board directed the superintendent to train a core of administration, staff, and the board, through the following steps:

1. The approach was to develop champion administrators and staff to develop the skills and common language of the model, and so on.
2. The teacher association (sometimes called the union) engaged in the training in support of the model.
3. Gain support of the media regarding research-based curriculum to improve student learning.

Research-Based School Correlates, Terminology, and Characteristics

As the school district began to speak about research-based schools, the staff, parents, and the community needed to know why the school district had made this decision about research-based curriculum.

Research-based schools have developed a series of characteristics to improve the education of children. Ronald Edmonds developed "Seven Correlates of Research-based Schools" (Effective Schools). This includes the following:

1. Instructional leadership
2. Clear and focused mission
3. Safe and orderly environment
4. Climate and high expectation
5. Frequent monitoring of student progress
6. Positive home-school relation
7. Opportunity to learn and student time on task[3]

As the staff became familiar with characteristics of effective schools, the following correlates were adopted in the North Thurston Public Schools:

1. Professional learning communities (PLCs)
2. Data teams
3. Teacher collaborative teams
4. Reflective practice
5. Continuous school improvement
6. Quality circles
7. Hedgehog concept[4]

When you apply the collective lists, you can see "why" Dr. Ronald Edmonds—cofounder of the Effective Schools movement—observed that public schools must make sure that children are successful:

We can, whenever and wherever we choose, successfully teach all children whose schooling is of interest to us. We already know more than we need to do that. Whether we do it must finally depend on how we feel about the fact that we haven't so far.

— Dr. Ronald Edmonds (1935–1983)

KEY AREA 2—DEVELOPING THE NEW STRATEGIC FRAMEWORK LEADERSHIP

The first portion of this chapter is a chronicle of the North Thurston Public Schools Board to develop a research-based curriculum of effective schools. The work of the board and the administration laid the groundwork for the second portion of the book. The work of the strategic framework focuses on the work of the board, administration, and the staff to

1. implement the curriculum work to improve the education for students;
2. implement the board's priorities and develop goals; and
3. engage the parents and the community in developing a trusting and compassionate community for the school district's work.

Superintendent's "Laser Focus" Leadership Work Plan

School districts periodically need to select a new superintendent. The North Thurston Public Schools faced this challenge in 2009. Earlier, the school district had adopted a research-based curriculum, undergone a complete school district audit, received the endorsement of the daily newspaper, and had begun the training of top administrators, teachers, and union leaders.

In effect, all the actions were important steps to take. Now, it was time for the board to select a new leader to move onto the next phase, growing improvement of student learning.

The board chose Raj Manhas as the superintendent. Raj Manhas—a business person and later an educator—was educated as an aeronautical engineer. He began his career in business and later became the Seattle School System superintendent. The board desired to continue to improve student performance while using student data as a resource to improve student education.

Setting the Direction of the New Superintendent

The first thing the board did was to meet with the new superintendent to discuss his direction. As a result, the school board endorsed the Strategic Framework for Leadership as the district leadership model.

The new strategic framework was designed to improve student learning and develop financial stability for the school district while developing a new culture of compassion for the school district and the community. The board's initiatives are discussed in four steps.

The strength of the superintendent was his skill in updating the board twice a year in the evaluation process. During the evaluation meetings, Raj Manhas, superintendent, presented a work plan that had multiple measures for the school district success.

First, the superintendent wanted to focus on data collection from the schools as a measure of student success. The evaluation process of the superintendent demonstrated his work plan. The superintendent reported to the board that the overall student performance was doing very well. However, the superintendent also told the board that some schools could do better in improving student performance in some subjects, especially mathematics. The superintendent's plan—from the board's perspective—took the following steps:

Step 1: The superintendent observed that some schools had not made the progress that he expected in comparison with similar schools statewide. The superintendent reported that he had developed an improvement planning process to address these areas. This priority would be the basis for supervising and evaluating principals.

Step 2: The superintendent employed a method recommended by Jim Collins. In his book, *Good to Great*, Collins wrote that an effective leader must make sure that managers who enter the bus—the organization—are seated in the right seat. He also noted that effective leaders confront the brutal facts. In fact, one administrator described the superintendent's leadership drive as laser-focused.

Step 3: The superintendent then brought in new administrators to monitor the performance of the principal and intervention services in each building and monitor student achievement. This resulted in several changes in the schools; for example, the superintendent made the following changes: three new elementary principals, two new middle school principals, and one new high school program that served 700 students. (Note: The school district later completed a boundary change for all the schools in the organization.)

Step 4: The superintendent told the school board that he wanted to make the North Thurston Public Schools a compassionate school system, with a high-performing administration, with proven student success, and a caring and supportive community.

The superintendent—by reporting to the board—performed the job by dealing with the operational expectations (traditional and Coherent Governance® models) of the school district—discussed in chapters one and two by monitoring principal performance and student learning results in the school district schools.

Second, the superintendent regularly briefed the board on school district successes. For example, the superintendent would show the board "the original, handwritten notes" that he wrote that described the board's direction to him. In effect, this was a way of affirming to the board, staff, and community: "This is my commitment to the board's goals for the school district."

The superintendent also reported to the school board that private-sector clients had congratulated the school district on its transparency. The superintendent had also been invited to join a private-sector hospital board of directors. The school district's goal was to be fully engaged in the community. The school district—in an earlier administration—changed its name from the "North Thurston School District" to "North Thurston Public Schools," as a way of saying to the owners that the schools belong to the public.

To memorialize his commitment to the board's goals, the superintendent transcribed his original notes from the board into a new strategic framework to implement student learning and engage the school, parents, and community.

Key Area 2: New Strategic Framework Leadership

The following material comes from North Thurston Public Schools' internal material and is used with permission:

> The goal of the strategic framework is to improve student learning, community engagement, trusting district, and compassionate culture.
>
> The new strategic framework is designed to improve student learning, develop financial stability to the school district while developing a new culture of compassion for the school district and the community.

STEP 1: BOARD'S SCHOOL DISTRICT PRIORITIES: STRATEGIC FRAMEWORK

> From the board's discussion with the superintendent and the district mission statement, the superintendent developed the strategic framework that included the following.[5]
>
> The school district mission statement says: "*Committed to excellence: Providing every student the academic and life skills necessary to succeed in a diverse world.*"
>
> By creating a strategic framework, [the] North Thurston Public Schools [wished] to create a simple, practical approach to annual planning which is both wholesome and grounded in reality. Many Focus Areas in this framework address multiple priorities. "We will use Key Performance indicators to evaluate our progress. The following elements guided the creation of this strategic framework. [Specifically, the portrait] of a North Thurston Public Schools'

graduate: Students in the North Thurston Public Schools have the following characteristics: creative, reflective, resilient, critical thinker, strong communicator, self-disciplined, compassionate, and globally aware."

School Board Priorities

1. Strategic focus area: Make student learning the center of everything we do. North Thurston Public Schools has a deeply rooted belief that all students can learn and grow. It is the responsibility of the entire school system to ensure the success of each and every student. The fundamental significance of this is making sure that every decision we make is focused on student learning. We will . . . provide proactive, system-wide processes where all staff shares responsibility for each student's progress, utilizing timely data to define, develop, and deliver rigorous, high quality, and engaging instruction. . . .

Focus Areas

(1) Implement a multi tiered system [RTI = Response to Intervention and PBIS = Positive-Based Intervention System] of support for both academics and social/emotional growth: Key performance indicators: state achievement tests.
(2) All students will meet or exceed state standards in math, English/language arts, and science on state assessment: key performance indicators: easy CBM data.
(3) All students will meet or exceed high school graduation requirements: key performance indicators: college and career readiness data.
(4) High schools will increase participation on SAT, Advanced Placement, and ACT tests.

2. Strategic focus area: Support the needs of the whole child.

North Thurston Public Schools will support the physical, social, and emotional needs of students and encourage mutual respect and effective collaboration among families, students, and staff. Addressing the needs of the whole child increases the likelihood of engagement in learning and high academic achievement for all students. . . .

Focus Areas

(1) All students will be provided a safe and caring learning environment that celebrates student diversity: key performance indicators: student attendance data.
(2) All students will have the social-emotional and academic supports necessary to be motivated and engaged in learning: key performance indicators: Washington State Healthy Youth Survey.

(3) Strategic focus area: Strengthen community engagement to support student learning.

North Thurston Public Schools is committed to strengthening transparent and varied community engagement and communication opportunities with the district's diverse populations. This open and honest communication will build trust with our families and community members and will encourage their involvement in supporting student learning and success. . . .

Focus Areas

. . .

(2) Create diverse and welcoming opportunities for citizen input and community engagement: key performance indicators: community and family engagement data.
(3) Collaborate with families, community partners, businesses, and volunteers to support student learning: key performance indicators: analytics for website, social media, and other communication tools.

. . .

4. Strategic focus area: Develop a trusting work culture through effective leadership and communication.

All North Thurston Public Schools employees will promote an authentic and trusting work culture by encouraging positive relationships that are respectful, compassionate, and collaborative. . . .

Focus Areas

. . .

(3) Recognize staff, students and community members for their NTPS achievements: key performance indicators: employee recognition data.
(4) Provide ongoing job-embedded professional development for staff: key performance indicators: employee feedback.

. . .

5. Strategic focus area: Be fiscally accountable and efficient in the use of public resources.

The North Thurston Public Schools will be good stewards of all resources entrusted to us by the public, providing the highest-quality services that are essential to supporting student learning. We will. . . [optimize] our resources for improved academic results and offer a transparent system that allows the public to hold us accountable.

. . .

Focus Areas

(1) The budget plan will be implemented, monitored and adjusted to ensure compliance: key performance indicators: maintain appropriate fund balance.
(2) All schools and departments will report activities that promote accountability and transparency: key performance indicators: preserve current bond ratings.

. . .

Step 2: School District Goals

The school district goals flow from the board's strategic framework. These goals are established annually. The board uses the goals as a measure of the superintendent's performance. The 2015–16 School District Goals include the following:

1. English Language Arts: The percent of students meeting standard on the grade level state assessment of Common Standards.
2. Mathematics: The percent of students meeting standard on the grade level state assessment of Common Core Standards in Mathematics.
3. Science: Students meet or exceed state grade level Common Core Standards in Science.
4. Student Support: Maintain student interventions for behavioral and social-emotional learning in grades K–12 so that there is a decrease in district-wide office behavioral referrals for defiance and non compliance.
5. Operational and Fiscal Effectiveness: Ensure processes are developed and implemented to improve system effectiveness. Provide the departmental support necessary to implement essential strategic projects.
6. Community Engagement: Inspire and build diverse community partnerships, strengthen family engagement in schools and deliver positive communication to help increase student learning and achievement.[6]

Goal 1: English Language Arts, Reading, and Writing

The district's goal is to fully implement the Common Core Standards for the English Language Arts.

The Common Core standards are focused strongly on a balance of literature and informational texts, as well as a greater focus on text complexity. In

Writing, there was a strong emphasis on argument and information/explanatory writing using evidence to inform an argument. . .

English and Social Studies teachers (grades 7–12) learned about and used the Classroom Based Assessments. The district took other initiatives in the following steps: Step 1: The teachers selected a new elementary reading curriculum for grades K–5 (e.g., professional development will be provided in the summer for the new elementary reading curriculum). Step 2: At the middle schools, teachers focused on professional development on "close reading" across content areas, while at the high school level teachers strengthened literacy groups in annotation, focusing on "close reading" and providing evidence.[7]

Goal 2: Math

The district implemented the Common Core Standards for Mathematics K–12. The district pursued with equal intensity conceptual understanding, procedural skill and fluency, and applications in math standards. At the elementary level, the district finished the final implementation of Stepping Stones K–5 in all schools and grades. At the middle school level, grades 6, 7, and 8 algebra was implemented by Engage New York, a Common Core-aligned curricula. Extended support opportunities exist at all levels, in and out of the school day.[8]

Goal 3: Science

The district is pursuing new science requirements. The transition to new science standards K–12 will be assessed in 2019. The standards include embedded science and engineering practices at each grade level and increasing the field study opportunities.

The district allocated time within the elementary day for science instruction for the 2015–16 school year. In another initiative, district aligned curriculum with Science, Technology, Engineering, and Math (STEM) goals while infusing mathematics, engineering, and technology where appropriate. It also embedded rich, real-world problems into curricula. This is particularly true for a STEM program centered in a high school.[9]

Goal 4: Student Support: Positive Behavioral Intervention Support (PBIS) in Three-Tiered Movement

The district-wide office discipline referrals for defiance/non compliance decreased by 5 percent from May 2014 to May 2015 as measured by School-wide Information Systems (SWIS) summary data. This met the 2014–15 district goal of a reduction in behavioral referrals for defiance/non compliance by

4 percent. District-wide office discipline referrals for defiance/non compliance decreased by 47 percent over the last three years.

Tier 1: Staff Training in Positive Based Instructional Strategies (PBIS)

The school district provided PBIS training in the 2014–15 school year to all bus drivers, custodians, cooks, cooks' helpers, and office professionals in addition to over twenty sessions of professional development on PBIS for administrators, teaching staff, and paraprofessionals.

Tier 2 PBIS Intervention: Student Mentoring

All schools are implementing the following Tier 2 PBIS interventions.

   Student mentoring, functional behavioral assessments, behavior contracts, and group social skill instruction. Students targeted for Tier 2 behavioral supports continue to improve. More than 52 percent of participants in elementary social skills groups increased their ability to handle conflict without aggression, which again highlighted impressive results: 72 percent of K–8 participants improved their ability to get along with peers, while 70 percent of students receiving mentoring have improved attendance, behavior, and academic performance.

Tier 3 PBIS Intervention: Parent Engagement in PBIS

More than 300 parents and children attended Military Mathematics Nights at six military grant-funded elementary schools. These events focused on promoting parent connection to the school, ways to improve math computation skills, and positive behavioral supports (PBIS training).[10]

Goal 5: Operational and Fiscal Effectiveness: Board Governance Leadership and Management Leadership

Compliance training for school and district staff began in the summer of 2014 and is ongoing in 2015–16. Two initiatives were also begun: (1) budget/staffing planning: a new coordinated system is on track and in progress, while (2) new accounting procedures are in place to streamline budget closing for 2014–15.[11]

Goal 6: Community Engagement

Community engagement is essential to the program for the district. The program provides ongoing programs and activities to promote transparent communication, strong community partnerships, a welcoming culture, and family engagement to support improved student learning.

Some examples of the community engagement activity include the following:

a. Communication plans for Common Core, Capital Facilities

    . . .

d. Compassionate Community Campaign (compassion coins, calendar, and service projects)

    . . .

g. 2,500 total volunteers; nearly 51,000 hours, averaging 900 unique volunteers per month

    . . .

The district extended the reach across social media, web, and smartphone (Facebook reach: 1,000 per post/5,850 likes; 1,200 Twitter followers; 4,500 NTPS app downloads; and 4,000 website users access website daily.)[12]

Step 3: Operational and Fiscal Effectiveness: Leadership/Management

Although similar to Goal 5, compliance training for school and district staff on operational and fiscal effectiveness began in the summer of 2014 and is ongoing in 2015–16. Specifically, the two initiatives were: (1) budget/staffing planning: a new coordinated system is on track and in progress, while (2) new accounting procedures are in place to streamline budget closing for 2014–15.[13]

In the case of the North Thurston Public Schools, the superintendent came out of a private sector—a banking career. The superintendent is very serious about making the school district a beacon of financial responsibility, and stability. When the superintendent arrived in the school district, the cash reserve was about $3 million dollars. After a six-year timeframe, the school district reserve amount is $16 million.

Even though the state has experienced a budget crisis, the district has put reserves into place through careful planning. The school district has implemented improvements in the school system; simultaneously, the school district has experienced student growth. The district passed a $175 million bond issue with 68 percent approval to build new schools, purchase a new private industry building, and improve other buildings. Moreover, the state will provide an additional amount of $50 million for support in building and improving schools.

Facilities Planning and Financing

Salish Middle School (WA)—a new middle school—is under construction with a $7 million savings. At the same time, a new boundary review process, which will result in a recommendation for new school boundaries to the board was completed. The board adopted the new boundary review.[14]

Technology Planning and Investment

The district developed a technology planning and investment program and purchases. In the 2013–14 school year, the district purchased and installed 975 Wireless Access Points throughout the district for full wireless coverage. The district has quadrupled bandwidth between schools to the cloud technology. The district added 900 laptops (30 carts) at elementary schools and replaced 277 non-mounted projectors with interactive projectors.

In all, the district is just a few hundred computers shy of doubling the number of computers. . . . The amount of supported end user devices in the schools compared to what it in the prior two years. The net gain of computers in two years is more than the previous ten years of adds combined.[15]

Customer Service Goal of Operational Departments

Internal staff satisfaction data indicates that 72.3 percent of our staff report being either "extremely" or "quite" satisfied with our operation services overall.[16]

Step 4: Collaborative Board and Superintendent Relations: Continuous Improvement through Continuous Meetings

Another initiative of the board is to engage the superintendent and administrators in continuous meetings throughout the year. Here is an example of continuous interactions through the year:

Board, Superintendent, and Administrators Goal Development and Progress Reports[17]

Year round planning for boards and administrators is an essential skill for school district leadership. Here is an example of year-round school district planning technique that establishes a schedule of dates for leadership activities.

Calendar of Leadership Activity

A calendar of leadership meetings—the board meeting with the administration—is vital for checking the progress toward meeting school district objectives:

- Early October: Principals present to the board a *School Improvement Plan* (SIP).
- Mid-October: Joint work session of the board, cabinet and City Council to share prominent programs for each jurisdiction.

- Mid-December: Board and cabinet work session on a selected topic.
- Early January: Goals progress discussion at Leadership Meeting (cabinet, directors, and principals).
- Mid-January: Superintendent's mid year performance review by the board.
- Early March: Second session with the principal's present progress toward *School Improvement Plans* (SIP).
- Mid-May: Second Joint Work Session of the board, cabinet and City Council.
- Mid-May: Goals progress review of district goals at the Leadership Meeting.
- Late May: Board and cabinet work session on designated topic.

KEY AREA 3—CHANGE IS CONSTANT: SEARCH FOR A NEW SUPERINTENDENT

With the retirement of Raj Manhas, the board began a search to select a new superintendent for the North Thurston Public Schools, Washington.

With the selection process of a new superintendent, the size of the school district that superintendents administer—a small district size versus a larger school district size—was an item of discussion.

In fact, some of the school district administrators came from small school districts who were involved in the process of superintendent selection. During the search process, a North Thurston administrator mentioned that there is a model for a superintendent job description called the "Dance Floor of the Superintendent's Job."

The model is fashioned from the rules of a dance floor and is designed to help a superintendent understand the difference between the size of school districts (small, medium, and large districts) and the administrative duties, responsibilities, and approaches to the various levels of management.

Size of the District Is an Important Management Consideration

The board and superintendent develop the district's goals. It requires the superintendent—through his or her operating expectations—to accomplish the goals and get results. The superintendent manages the district and will move through the various rings of the dance floor to manage the school district and educate the whole child.

In smaller school districts, the superintendent will be more engaged in a variety of functions and activities of their jobs as is represented by the various rings of the school district dance floor model. Simply put, this is caused by the sheer size of the school district.

In larger school districts, however, the cabinet and the directors allow the superintendent to delegate specific responsibilities and tasks. Although the superintendent can move among the various rings—and frequently does to maintain morale—there must be consideration by the superintendent for the roles that are delegated so that a feeling of distrust among various administrators, with delegated responsibility at each level, does not emerge.

In effect, the superintendent must be able to apply another management skill: reading the pulse of the organization and staff. This model can assist a superintendent who comes from a smaller school district to take responsibility to manage a district that is larger.

For the North Thurston Public Schools, the board selected Debra Clemens. She comes to the North Thurston job (14,000 students) from a smaller school district—4,000 students.

Large School District Dance Floor Model

For purposes of a larger school district, let's assume a dance floor model with five rings that circle. Here are the rules as they apply to the superintendent job role. The dancers (district administrators/staff) always dance in a counter clockwise direction, based on the governance goals/results developed by the board for the district.

Each ring represents a line of responsibility, as you can see in figure 18.1 on p. 159. The dance floor direction is counterclockwise, with the speed of the outer ring, and moving more slowly to the center position of the superintendent.

The outer ring of the dance floor (5) identifies the area in which the fast-moving staff work (teachers and classified employees), providing instruction and services to students.

The next inner ring of the dance floor (4) identifies the area in which the work of the principal administers the school and supervises the students and staff.

The next inner ring of the dance floor (3) identifies the area in which the work of the directors (finance, human relations, construction, food, etc.) has specific administrative functions.

The next inner ring of the dance floor (2) identifies the area in which the work of the cabinet (assistant superintendents, instruction, leadership, accounting, community engagement, etc.) has a direct relationship with the superintendent and performs a specific administrative function.

The center of the dance floor (1) identifies the area occupied by the superintendent who has a direct relationship with the board and administers the district with all staff and services.

The superintendent is expected to move among the various rings and engage staff tactfully at all levels. It is often spoken of as Management of Business by Wandering Around (MBWA).

Dance Floor of The Superintendent's Job

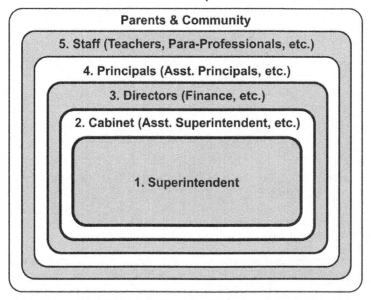

Figure 18.1.   Dance Floor of the Superintendent's Job. Copyright © 2016, Chuck Namit, Strategem LLC, Values Governance®

Breaking Bread Together Work Session Dinner

In May of the school year, the district holds an annual Breaking Bread Together Work Session Dinner for the board and cabinet. The purpose of the work session is to discuss some of the instructional and operational program elements that have been implemented and their effect on coming goals or elements that haven't yet been implemented.

Also, as a part of the transition, the board, the superintendent, and the cabinet discuss the transition schedule for the new superintendent.

Here is the Board and Cabinet Work Session Dinner Agenda:

Tuesday, May x, 20xx: _____Restaurant (Private Room)

1. Leadership Update & Discussion

   a. Superintendent Transition
   b. District/School Leadership Updates

2. Instructional Update & Discussion
3. Operations (Expectation) Update & Discussion
4. Public Relations (Community Engagement) Update & Discussion
5. Reflections/Questions/Discussion

The board and cabinet group motto: The group that works together stays together.

Final Thoughts on Governance and Management

School board governance and superintendent leadership must focus on a school district's product or service: (1) increasing student achievement and success, (2) building future schools, and (3) maximizing operational efficiency.

Unless the school board and superintendent take action to address student achievement, it has failed in its mission. In a report entitled "Protect Children, Protect Our Future," the United States Environmental Protection Agency (EPA) summed it up this way: "Children are 30% of the world population, but 100% of our future."

What We've Learned in the Application-Opportunity

Theme: A board's chief responsibility is to create an efficient governing system that improves student learning and achievement.

Every school board member must answer this question: Why do you serve on your board? I believe the answer should be to improve a student's achievement in our schools. So what are the steps to improve curriculum and instruction?

Step 1: The board must determine that students have an excellent curriculum. Typically a research firm can do an audit of the school district curriculum and report its findings to the board, school district leadership, staff, and the community.

Step 2: Based on the consultant audit of the school district, the superintendent devises a plan for the board's school district priorities called the strategic framework to improve learning, community engagement, and trusting district and community culture.

Step 3: When a school board must change school district administrative leadership, choose a superintendent who is responsible for improving student performance, and provide finances and resources for the school district.

Chapter 19

Board Member Communication: Four Communication Styles

Part 1: Reviewing the Essential Skills

Step 6A: Values Governance® System

Communication Style

Communication among board members is an important aspect of governing a school district; therefore, board members should gain an understanding of their own style and that of their fellow board members. In chapter 9, we provided a Communication Style Survey, which simulates the Myers-Briggs communication instrument, for each board member to take. This survey will help board members and the CEO reveal their communication behavior.

Since board members and the CEO have different communication styles, this will assist in communicating with one another.

Communication Style Survey[1]

In chapter 9, when you identified your communication style, you found that your dominant communication style is sensor (S), intuition (I), thinker (T), or feeler (F).

Interpreting Your Communication Style Survey Score

Your highest score will indicate your dominant communication style. The next highest score will indicate your secondary communication style (see table 19.1).

Table 19.1.   Communication Style

RELATIONSHIP FOCUS		
A S S E R T I V E	*Intuition*[2a] Characteristics: • **Directive** • **Energetic**	*Feeler*[2b] Characteristics: • **Congenial** • **Judicious**	C O O P E R A T I V E
	Sensor[2c] Characteristics: • **Determinative** • **Purposeful**	*Thinker*[2d] Characteristics: • **Investigative** • **Organized**	
TASK FOCUS		

Source: Adapted material from "Find out How Your Journal Personality May Be at Odds," *Working Smart,* The Executive Service from Learning International, vol. 3, no. 1, January 1986. Copyright © 2016, Chuck Namit, Strategem LLC, Values Governance®

The elements in the table 19.1 break down as follows:

1. Italicized type is the Communications Style Survey instrument language that simulates the Myers-Briggs instrument (e.g., intuition).
2. Under each of the styles (e.g., intuition), you'll note the characteristics of each style (e.g., directive, energetic), which will give you further insight into the style.

Each board member must complete the Communication Style Survey instrument and then it is time to review table 19.1.

The communication windows determine the elements that describe an individual's type of communication.

Now the board members—in this Application-Opportunity chapter—need to examine the potential strengths and weaknesses of the four styles—intuition, thinker, feeler, and sensor. This identifies the behavioral styles of each board member as they work together to improve their governance style. The Values Governance® system requires board members to collaborate and work together as a team.

Part 2: Implementing Advanced Application and Opportunity

Key Area 1—Four Communication Styles: Potential Strengths and Weaknesses

Swiss psychoanalyst Carl Jung developed a theory that people had four main psychological types to process data (receive messages) and communicate (send messages). He maintained that these four levels of user preference (or communication channels) change very little from childhood to adulthood.

You have probably asked these questions: Why do individuals see, act, and say things differently than I do? Or you might have opined: if only they could see things the way I do, things would be better!

Researchers Isabel Myers and Katherine Briggs (1875–1968) took Jung's work and turned it into an inventory of behavior styles to make the best match of a person to a job during World War II. It is now widely used in the private and public sectors. The scale does not purport to be the same as the famous Myers-Briggs Type Indicator scale. However, the "Four Communication Styles" scale attempts to approximate the famous scale by giving you some indication of your propensity to use one of the four styles as your dominant behavior, communication pattern, or style.[2]

Let's break down the various behavior-communication styles and look at the characteristics, potential strengths, and weaknesses of each.

The Intuition

People with intuition behavior display the following communication elements:

1. Characteristics: They tend to imagine, conceive, envision, visualize, fantasize, daydream, suppose, abstract, reckon, create, innovate, and so on.
2. Potential strengths: They are abstract, concept-oriented, and able to link intuitive thoughts. They are forward-thinking. They have a tendency to create from the various parts into the whole; what Disney calls "*imagineering*." Their time orientation is the future. Therefore, future tense is their language. They are green-hat thinkers and creative team members.
3. Potential weaknesses: They are criticized for being too blue sky, impractical.
4. Communication approach: They begin with the end in mind; therefore, start with an overview and explain what the result will be. They have intuition, value innovation and creativity, and never want to be in the valley of detail.

The Thinker

People with thinker behavior display the following communication elements:

1. Characteristics: They tend to deduct, rationalize, generalize, infer, conclude, reason, calculate, compute, recap, derive, extrapolate, order data, project, deduce, surmise, summarize, analyze, review, encapsulate, epitomize, and so on.
2. Potential strengths: They are data oriented. They relate to the environment of their world by cautiously thinking through things. "I'm logical" is their

defense (e.g., "haste makes waste"). They analyze and then act. Their motto is: "Work it out." Their time orientation is the past, present, and the future, as long as it is on a factual point of view.
3. Potential weaknesses: They are criticized as being nitpicking, being rigid. Their role is to wear the black hat, or "why it can't work."
4. Communication approach: They play the role of Joe Friday and say, "Just the facts!" As a thinker, they want the organization to use data to prove the point.

The Feeler

People with feeler behavior display the following communication elements:

1. Characteristics: They tend to relate, feel, empathize, engage, sympathize, and understand. They identify with other people by rapport building, connecting, bonding, resonating, trusting, linking, harmonizing, evoking, and so on.
2. Potential strengths: They are people oriented. They express their feelings about what is happening. They can read the morale of the group. They use social bonding to reach their goal in working the environment and developing personal relations. They use interpersonal skills to communicate. The feeler adjusts to the emotions or moods of others. They are more informal and casual and pictures of family abound. Their time orientation is the past (e.g., into nostalgia and memorabilia).
3. Potential weaknesses: They tend to be criticized for being too soft, not hard-nosed enough, and touchy-feely.
4. Communication approach: A meeting with a feeler should begin with some degree of informality. The presenter should show the impact that an idea will have on people.

The Sensor

People with sensor behavior display the following communication elements:

1. Characteristics: They are people who act, react, do, sense, compete, attain, overtake, occupy, perform, stage, take control, enact, electrify, equip, strive for results, contend, combat, and so on.
2. Potential strengths: They are criticized for being action oriented. They deal with the world through their senses. They are hardworking and able to take command and handle a lot of work. They have a high energy level, with high achievement orientation. They will go to battle to meet goals and get results. They are short-tempered, with the motto: "So get to the point." Their time orientation is the here and now.

3. Potential weaknesses: Sensors are short sighted, in a hurry, not thinking things through; exhibit poor planning; and are often seen as being rude to others.
4. Communication approach: Sensors are spring-loaded, action-oriented people. Therefore, they can be direct and get to the point quickly. Remember: If you waste a sensor's time, they'll have no time for you or your idea.

Chapter 20

Knowing Your Governance Style: Implications for Better School Governance

CHAPTER APPLICATION-OPPORTUNITY H

Part 1: Reviewing the Essential Skills

Step 6B: Values Governance® System (Continued)

Governance Profile Scale (GPS)

At this point, if board members want to establish a new governance process, they must establish their policy control status by determining whether they are task-focused, moderate, or relationship-focused by taking the Governance Profile Scale (GPS) survey, presented in chapter 9. The Values Governance® system—in this Application-Opportunity chapter—requires board members to study their governance profile, observations, and applications.

The Governance Profile Scale (GPS) Score

Count the numbers in each of the ten questions and list the total score below. When you have your GPS number you can then identify your tendency to relationship-focused, moderate, or task-focused policy development. If your number is not precisely listed, modify to the nearest number to fit your GPS scale/score.

List actual GPS score: _____. List policy tendency (relationship-focused, moderate, or task-focused): _____.

The GPS instrument will give you a good idea of your governance style, whether you are task-focused, moderate, or relationship-focused as indicated in your governance style in policy development.

Bull's-Eye Approach: Establishing Policy Control Status

The board can use the bull's-eye approach, which makes the board feel more comfortable with the policies and the degree of control. Specifically, it's a way to think of the layering of policies. An example of a bull's-eye is used to indicate the degrees of policy control. (See figure 20.1.) Each policy layer—as you move toward the center of the bull's-eye—represents a higher level of policy control.

The bull's-eye has two functions. First, imagine the arrow gauge at the bottom of the model, which shifts the degree of control, demonstrates the maximum degree of control by the board as you move to the center of the bull's-eye. Second, the reverse is also true: specifically, the board, at some subsequent time, reduces its control over a policy area by eliminating policies and moves to the outer ring (away from the center of the bull's-eye).

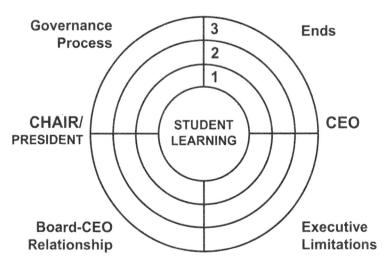

Rings of Control
Determined by the Board Through
Any Reasonable Interpretation

Any Reasonable Interpretation (ARI)

Figure 20.1.   Rings of Control Determined by the Board through Any Reasonable Interpretation. *Source*: Adapted material from John Carver & Miriam Mayhew Carver, Reinventing Your Board (Jossey-Bass Inc., 1997). Copyright © 2016, Chuck Namit, Strategem LLC, Values Governance®

The bull's-eye model of your policy control is a measure of your board members' personal behavior. For example, the policy control rings' status is as follows:

1. Inner Ring: Task-focused policy control ring
2. Middle Ring: Moderate policy control ring
3. Outer Ring: Relationship-focused policy control ring

Board Must Come to Agreement on Policy Control Status

Once each board member has taken the policy control status, then it's time to establish the board's agreement on its policy status.

As we've mentioned, a board's policy control status can change over time. One consideration is the board's comfort with its control of the school district governance. For example, if the board has concerns over school district budget status, it may need more control over the administration of the district. On the other hand, the board may be comfortable with the superintendent's management and achievement of the school district.

A Skilled Consultant Can Be Useful

A final thought: Many times the use of a skilled consultant or facilitator can be useful in the discussion about an individual board member's GPS and the determination of the board's GPS.

Part 2: Implementing Advanced Application and Opportunity

Key Area 1—Governance Profile Observations and Applications[1]

Here are some questions that board members can use to examine their GPS. It is important for the board members to discuss their GPS survey to develop a consensus within the board. Let's look at your response:

1. Were you surprised and/or comfortable with the results of the GPS?
2. What have you learned about yourself from the GPS?
3. In what ways would acknowledgment of individual GPSs of your fellow board members assist you in your board service?
4. How would you use the GPS to help your board better govern your school district?
5. Has your board identified its tendency toward relationship-focused, moderate, or task-focused policy development?
6. In the next thirty days, what can you do to help your board become better governors of your school district?

KEY AREA 2—FOCUS-ON-THE-BOARD EXERCISE[2]

With the information we have learned about one another, let's take some time to determine what the board can do to become more effective as a collective school board.

Let's Dialogue about Issues the Board Faces

Directions: Complete the following statements in the space provided. Then share your perceptions with your fellow board members, superintendent, and the community.

1. Members of this board are energized by the following action(s):

   List the various actions (e.g., less funding from the state, federal government):

   a. _____
   b. _____
   c. _____
   d. _____
   e. _____

2. My board seems to prefer information that is presented in the following manner:

   a. _____
   b. _____
   c. _____
   d. _____
   e. _____

3. My board's decision making criteria tend to be:

   a. _____
   b. _____
   c. _____
   d. _____
   e. _____

4. The way my board usually governs is (traditional governance, Policy Governance®, Coherent Governance®, Values Governance®, or some other governance structure variable). Now here are some questions that the board and the superintendent need to discuss:

a. How well does the board govern based on the board self-assessment?
b. How well does the superintendent manage the district based on the superintendent evaluation?
c. How well does our district engage the community in school activities?
d. Do the board and superintendent meet with the city council?
e. Does the board believe the district goals have been met?

5. The board and superintendent discuss the organization of regular link-age meetings with the community. What are the topics brought up by the community?
6. Discuss some steps the board should take to better govern and be more effective.
7. We agree to certain actions to help improve our effectiveness as a board and superintendent.

   a. Board Self-Assessment:
   b. Superintendent Evaluation:
   c. Community Engagement:
   d. Linking with the Community:

Board's Commitment to Action

What is the board willing to commit to as district action? Use table 20.1 to commit to the school district action. Upon completion of the action plan, the board must return to energizing the community (discussed on pages 170–171).

Table 20.1.   Action Plan: Now What Do We Do?

Discussion Item	Board Issue/ Action	Supt. Issue/ Action	Contact Whom/ Which Group	Action Plan Design
1.				
2.				
3.				
4.				
5.				
6.				
7.				
8.				
9.				
10.				

Design Action Plan Steps

The board and superintendent design the action plan for implementation:

Action Steps

1. _____

    a. By whom: _____

    b. Action date: _____

2. _____

    a. By whom: _____

    b. Action date: _____

3. _____

    a. By whom: _____

    b. Action date: _____

4. _____

    a. By whom: _____

    b. Action date: _____

5. _____

    a. By whom: _____

    b. Action date: _____

Chapter 21

High-Performing Community Engagement Techniques

CHAPTER APPLICATION-OPPORTUNITY I

Part 1: Reviewing the Essential Skills

Step 7: Values Governance® System

An effective board wants to establish internal and external linkage with the community. In this Application-Opportunity chapter on community engagement, we offer two high-powered techniques of school-community engagement projects to improve school-community engagement.

Part 2: Implementing Advanced Application and Opportunity

The two high-powered community engagement approaches are the nitty-gritty of the Values Governance® approach to fully engaging the community in improving student learning. Since these high-powered community engagement techniques are extensive, we will cover each project in separate sections:

Project 1: School-Community Engagement Institute (on page 177)
Project 2: Ten-Step Community Engagement Facilitated Planning Model (on page 179)
These high-powered projects can be used individually or paired or use all techniques in a planned program.

KEY AREA 1—DECODING STAKEHOLDER COMMUNICATION

The Values Governance® system is clear that one of the most important approaches in a school district is to be very involved in performing community engagement activities. This community engagement is key to developing a process of listening to and engaging the community on increasing student learning and school improvement.

Communication research says that selective perception and selective retention of communication can be either filtered (received or resisted) or coded by groups and group opinion leaders (Everett Rogers and Joseph Klapper) to meet the needs of stakeholder groups. To apply this research, you can use the analogy of coded communication. To crack the code of communication allows an individual or organization to understand themselves and others, particularly the owners of your organizations.

Cracking the Communication Code Principles

A book by Thom Hartmann, *Cracking the Code: How to Win Hearts, Change Minds, and Restore America's Original Vision*, gives some insights on how to crack the communication code that surrounds many stakeholder groups.

Hartmann unlocks the secret of cracking the communication code with the following principles:

1. When we communicate, feeling comes first. Emotions will always trump intellect, at least in the short term.[1]
2. Well-formed outcomes are desirable. If we're going to set out to change another person's behavior by changing his or her mind about something, we want the outcome of that new behavior to be useful to that person, us, and everything and everybody else involved.[2]
3. We add tools but never take away tools. People will always be receptive to new options, new tools, and new behaviors. It's always more effective to say "start this" than to say "stop that."[3] We will discuss this technique of new tools and new behavior later in the chapter.
4. There are no failures, only feedback; no mistakes, only outcomes. When we understand the results of our actions as "feedback" and "outcomes," new spectrums of options for learning open up to us.[4]

Telling the Organization's Story

Hartmann says that you communicate most effectively when you tell engaging stories. He calls a story a "map." Each map has a different "territory."

The "territory" refers to the point of view or perspective of the storyteller. Therefore, a person tells each story or map with a different "territory," which is another person's reality or perspective. So, each person's story is a different piece of reality.

All this leads to Hartmann's final communication code principle—the principle of storytelling:

> The key to effective communication is to find the best story to use to convey your understanding of the world to the greatest number of people.[5]

Surely, school board members and administrators are familiar with telling the school district's story. Hartmann's advice comes into play by applying the communication code principles to the stories you tell to the stakeholders and owners about their schools.

KEY AREA 2—HELP MODELS AND COMMUNITY ENGAGEMENT PROCESSES

Here is an example of how the board can bring community/business/college leaders together to develop help models, while also developing a community engagement process. It is important that the programs include many elements to help current students and reengage dropout students:

a. Academic instruction, which includes GED preparation and academic skills as well as college and work readiness
b. Instruction by certified teachers, college instructors, paraprofessionals, and workforce instructors
c. Case management, counseling, and resource and referral services
d. Opportunity for qualified students to enroll in tuition-free college courses and work preparation opportunities[6]

Another important element in developing a process to better improve the educational outcomes for students—whether the program is at the district level or the state level—is to identify the components and systems that students will face in improving their opportunities. Here is a list:

- Business sector
- Justice systems
- Postsecondary education systems (community colleges and colleges)
- Adult education systems
- Philanthropic sector
- Government sector

- K–12 education systems
- Child welfare systems
- Nonprofits[7]

The board—with the assistance of the administration—can invite the leaders/stakeholders to a conference or a workshop. A consultant might be hired to lead the workshop in the following processes:

a. Engage key community/business/college/workplace leaders and stakeholders: You must reach out to the groups to help with the first step.
b. Create a common agenda: The difference between the current situation and gaining a common vision is gaining a consensus on what needs to happen.
c. Mapping special audiences: A school district can map the location of special needs families and students in the school district. This mapping process is a strategy to identify locations of special audiences and thereby provide help to organizations with the locations and the special audiences.
d. Identify the needs and helping resources within the community: The board, administration, and community/business/workplace leaders engage in the process of identifying the needs and resources needed to help students. This process allows community leaders to emerge. The need is for new leadership to develop the basis for helping community outreach.[8]

KEY AREA 3—HIGH ENERGY SCHOOL-COMMUNITY ENGAGEMENT PROJECTS

Just as a school district must develop its own governance culture, a community—with special audiences such as target stakeholders, clients, active civic groups, and news media—must develop a culture of community engagement.

Two different projects can assist a school district in developing a culture in the community that supports school district needs and activities. The first project is the development of a Community Engagement Institute. This is essential for creating the culture or environment of engagement with the public.

A former bank—Washington Mutual Bank—gave a grant to the Washington State School Directors' Association (WSSDA) to have six school districts develop a school-community engagement project. The study formulated an approach that school districts can employ to develop a culture of community engagement. Here is a project of the School-Community Engagement Institute:

Project 1: School-Community Engagement Institute[9]

Here is the two-day agenda for the School-Community Engagement Institute:

DAY 1: FRIDAY MORNING SESSION

9:00 Purpose of Institute: Engaging parents and the community as stakeholders to improve student learning
Introduction of faculty and school district teams: roles of school boards, staff, parents, and community members
9:15 Educational reform and the need for community support
10:00 Community engagement: an overview:

1. Why community engagement?
2. How and why school boards and school districts engage communities in policy level issues, setting the district's direction and implementing key initiatives?
3. What we know about effective community engagement (Karen L. Mapp's research found in chapter 7)?

10:30 Break
10:45 District challenges to authentic community engagement: case studies
ACTIVITY: Identify Each District's Challenge/Issue around Which to Engage the Community (communication wall facilitation [CWF] technique is used to capture and record district team discussion)
11:20 ACTIVITY: Teams Share Community Engagement Challenges/Success Stories
11:55 Introduction to afternoon session
12:00 Lunch (mix, network, and sit with other team members)
DAY 1: FRIDAY AFTERNOON SESSION
1:00 Overview of community engagement models and strategies: from policy and district-wide community engagement to school-family partnerships
1:15 Knowing your community
1. Asset mapping to identify key stakeholders and communicators/opinion leaders
2. Engaging cultural and ethnic communities
1:40 ACTIVITY: Knowing Your Community (CFW)
2:05 Strategies for listening to your community
1. Surveys, polls, and assessments
2. Focus groups
3. Future search conference
4. Appreciative inquiry

2:30 ACTIVITY: Teams Discuss How They Might Use Listening Strategies (CFW)

   3:00 Break

   3:15 Models for engaging the community in conversation:

1. Small group conversation
2. Café chat
3. Study circle

   3:50 Models for school-family partnerships:

1. Building relationships for student success (Northwest Regional Educational Laboratory)
2. Family-friendly schools (WA Alliance for Better Schools)

Presenters provide brief descriptions of the models and engage district teams in a short activity to get a "taste" of the models. Presenters will also be available during "homework" session to answer questions and explain the models.

   4:50 Brief introduction to community engagement planning process (preview of Saturday's session)

Homework assignment: Community asset mapping for identifying and communicating with key stakeholders (CFW)

   5:05 Recess: Dinner on your own (team and facilitator)

   6:30 Homework—Community asset mapping developed by each district

   8:30 Team (BLT Technique = Boot Leg Time)

DAY 2: SATURDAY MORNING SESSION

   9:00 ACTIVITY: Share Community Asset Mapping—Key Findings

   9:45 Introduction to next steps to engage your community around your district's identified issue

   10:00 Community engagement plan template: Train-the-Trainer model

   10:15 Break

   10:30 Facilitated team practice session: Planning to address identified issue around which to engage community

Goal: Take one of the issues (or subissues) and work through the ten-step process (teams/facilitators):

1. Review community asset map and environmental scan analysis
2. Frame the issue to address
3. Identify goal(s) for community engagement to address issue(s)
4. Identify community engagement strategy(-ies) for meeting goal(s)
5. Clarify roles of team members

6. Identify other people to involve
7. Assess resources needed
8. Develop activity timeline
9. Develop an evaluation process to measure success
10. Celebrate success with community/stakeholders

Facilitators work with teams to practice the planning process and utilize forms and CFW.

12:00 Lunch (mix, network, and sit with other team members)

1:00 Facilitated team practice session, continued (teams/facilitators)

2:00 Next steps in planning at the district level:

1. Determine further technical assistance needs
2. Identify next steps—program publicity and kickoff activity
3. Plan for implementation of next steps (teams/facilitators)

3:00 ACTIVITY: Teams Report on Progress (CFW)

3:50 Closing: Evaluation

4:00 Adjourn (next session in the school district is with targeted groups)

The School-Community Engagement Institute's final goal: Set a date in six months for a follow-up meeting.

Another planning tool for the school-community engagement group is a Ten-Step Community Engagement: Facilitated Planning Model. This model covers a template for consistent and reliable community engagement. Again, here is an exercise that can help a school district plan its effort:

Project 2: Ten-Step Community Engagement: Facilitated Planning Model[10]

The second effective project of a community engagement project is to implement a Ten-Step Community Engagement Facilitated Planning Model that is used as a community engagement plan template. This is the second step used in the Values Governance® system to energize the community by the planning process.

Step 1: Review Community Asset Map and Environmental Scan Analysis

You can develop a Future Scan: Internal and External Environmental Analysis process. This process includes the following categories:

a. Strengths and opportunities
b. Weaknesses and threats
c. Trends
d. Resources

The follow-up assignments include the following:

a. Additional data needed
b. Who's responsible
c. Timelines for implementation
d. Effected completion dates
e. Special criteria, requirements

Step 2: Frame the Issue(s) to Be Addressed

The effectiveness of community engagement depends on defining the issues. An effective technique is to identify the issue(s) and subissue(s). Here's an example:

District issue: 1. Engage the community/stakeholders on an initiative to improve student achievement through the implementation of an Effective Schools' research model in school districts.

District subissues:

a. School board adopts a five-year plan to implement the Effective Schools initiative, replete with a plan to unpack the initiative through an implementation plan.
b. Change in the school day and calendar to provide in-service training for staff with the late start Wednesday of schools.
c. Determine the impact of the late start Wednesday of schools on parents, regarding safety issues and the increased cost and use of daycare.

Step 3: Identify Goal(s) for the Community Engagement to Address Issue(s)

Goals are statements that define or outline what you want to achieve. Goals are often called bite-sized steps that assist you in defining a vision, an initiative, a program, or a project.

Delineate your goals as SMART goals: This acronym comes from the following:

Specific
Measurable
Achievable
Realistic
Time-phased

Step 4: Identify Community Engagement Strategies for Meeting Goals

Surely, the development of strategies can provide skills and expertise through involvement with many of the following activities:

a. Focus groups typically involve eight to twelve people, with a cross section of the community represented. A skilled, neutral facilitator or moderator leads the discussion on various topics such as recent graduation rates.
b. Community forums or town hall meetings may attract from 60 to 200 people. These meetings focus on a hot topic such as "concern over high-stake testing" or "what would the ideal school look like."
c. A study circle involves ten to fifteen participants, which includes students, teachers, parents, and patrons. The purpose of a study circle is to create a dialogue and arrive at a decision about an issue or concern.
d. High-level advisory committees and the superintendent leadership councils are made up of a cross section of the community and business interests that meet periodically and offer guidance on various issues affecting the schools and the community.[11]

Step 5: Clarify Roles of Team Members

Team roles need to be defined. Here are some characteristics that you can use to identify the role of team members. Here are a baker's dozen of role attributes:

- Fully prepares for and attends the meeting (please turn off all cell phones)
- Fully participates by offering ideas
- Offers enthusiasm that helps create a positive climate
- Accepts and completes assignments
- Actively engages in group discussions and processes
- Creatively develops ideas
- Provides solutions
- Helps implement solutions
- Helps develop and participate in presentations
- Keeps a commitment to the group's aims and goals
- Fosters and adheres to a code of collaboration
- Collects data and bases decision(s) on data
- Communicates progress of the school district with influentials from their sphere of influence.[12]

Step 6: Identify Other People to Involve

You can develop a Key Opinion Leader Checklist by identifying opinion leaders and by creating a list of categories of community positions. For example, here are some of the included categories:

- Corporate involvement program participant
- Charitable organization volunteer leader
- Business leader

- Community leader
- Professional association leader
- Youth leaders
- Other (specify): _____

List the name for each category. Then create columns for the following information:

- Category for the opinion leader
- Name of opinion leader
- Contact person
- Specific objective of the contact
- Follow-up to contact

When developing the Key Opinion Leader Checklist, be certain to capture the cultural richness of your community. For example, consider race, gender, cultural, and ethnic diversity in your selections.

Step 7: Assess Resources Needed

An innovative way to dig up and create assets is to map the conduits of innovation as potential resources. To map the conduits of innovation within your state use these categories to analyze your state's change factors:

a. Identify the innovators: List for each category the opinion leaders and innovators in your state.

    1. Business
    2. Government
    3. Education
    4. Media
    5. Community

b. Identify the trendsetting institutions and districts: List the trendsetting institutions and districts for each of the locations indicated.
c. Location of the trendsetter within the state:

    East
    West
    North
    South

d. Description of the institution or district:

    Rural
    Urban
    Suburban

e. Relationships of trendsetters: Define the relationship of trendsetting institutions in letter b to the categories that are listed.

1. List name(s) submitted
2. Workforce
3. Location
4. Partnership one another (specify)

f. Patterns of innovation and change: List the various types of industry within your state:

1. Traditional industries: for example, low-tech, low-skilled, and high-labor industries
2. Technologically based industries: for example, high-tech, high-skilled, education-centered industries

g. Forging new linkages: If you could form a new relationship that would "incubate" desired innovation and change (e.g., business and universities as partnerships to incubators of change):

1. What would it look like?
2. Who would be the players?
3. What outcome would be preferred?

Step 8: Develop Summative Worksheet and Activity Timeline

A summative worksheet is crucial to the follow-through and implementation of your community engagement efforts. Here are the elements of a summative worksheet and activity timeline. Include these categories in the worksheet:

a. Community engagement issue(s) and subissue(s) defined
b. Goal statements
c. Strategies that cut across goals
d. Action steps needed to implement
e. Person assigned to implement
f. Needed resources
g. Key dates for implementation
h. Evaluation

Step 9: Evaluate Your Community Engagement Effort

The evaluation motto: If it is worth doing, it is worth evaluating.

Step 10: Celebrate with Community Stakeholders

Never forget to celebrate success. It's a psychological closure to an event or a task.

Community engagement is essential to school communities—the school-community engagement techniques develop a cultural relationship with the community. The community's schools and our kids become our future.

What We've Learned in the Application-Opportunity

Theme: The board's role in providing community engagement to the governance process is vital in becoming a successful public school system. The high-performing community engagement processes engage the community in what we have called a whole governance model.

1. In the traditional method of describing a typical school board, the community elects trustees to represent them in running the schools. An organization chart shows the community at the top with elected representatives sitting on a board. They would hire a superintendent who operates the schools. In essence, this is the method that most of 14,000 public schools use to run their organization. However, the Values Governance® system encourages school districts to use the Listening Linkage and Energizing the Community processes.

2. High-energy techniques of school-community engagement projects give the school district ways to involve the community.

3. The Two-Way Linkage and Energizer Processes engages the full governance approach that is needed to have effective schools.

Chapter 22

Turning to the Values Governance® System

CHAPTER APPLICATION-OPPORTUNITY J

Part 1: Reviewing the Essential Skills

Step 8: Values Governance® System

The Values Governance® model uses elements of the traditional governance model and adds other elements of the alternative governance models. Specifically, the Values Governance® model uses the Green-Line model—utilizing the division authority role definition with the 9:00 and 3:00 line—identifying the board domain above the line and the administrative domain below the line. In a broad perspective, this is the role definition of the board and the superintendent.

But the board is also responsible for the global direction of the school district. Specifically, the Values Governance® model adds the four categories found in the alternative governance models, as follows:

- Governance Procedures: The culture of the school district from staff treatment, officers' (CEO, CFO) roles, and so on.
- Board-Superintendent-CEO Relations: The board's relationship with the superintendent that includes monitoring of CEO performance, delegation of CEO authority, and so on.
- Operational Procedures: The board's monitoring of the work of the superintendent in the operational expectations of the school district, as well as human relations, budget, and financial management, and so on.
- Goals: The board's direction for the school district as delineated in goals, results of student achievement, and so on.

The Values Governance® model also identifies two key elements in reviewing the leadership of school district.

- Board Self-Assessment: The board process includes the elements of the governance procedure and the board-superintendent-CEO Relations.
- Superintendent-CEO Evaluation: The board evaluates the superintendent's performance in the areas of operational procedures and meeting goals.

This Application-Opportunity chapter presents the Jumping-the-Canyon method of introducing the Values Governance® system to a school district.

Part 2: Implementing Advanced Application and Opportunity

Key Area—Jumping to a New Values Governance® System

You can improve governance of the school district with several concrete governance changes discussed in earlier chapters (see figure 22.1, the Values Governance model).

1. Define the roles of the chief governance officer (CGO) and chief executive officer (CEO) as the parallel leaders to form the leadership team: John Carver originally identified the leader of the organization as the CEO. With the term of the CEO, policies are determined by the board to identify expectations and authority. Educators, of course, use the term "superintendent" to identify the CEO. Other public organizations identify the executive director or mayor as the CEO. The policies for the CEO effectively define the role and designation of the superintendent. Values Governance® expands governance to a team by proposing the concept of parallel leadership and adding the role of the chairperson or president of the board as the CGO. The CGO leads the governance team, while the CEO leads the management team. The governance team and the management team are called the leadership team. With the role definitions of the board and the superintendent, you have modernized the leadership team that will lead the new Values Governance® system.
2. Implement a monitoring system to better evaluate the performance of the CEO or superintendent: Periodic monitoring helps improve the performance of the superintendent, as well as the school district performance. Chapter 5 describes how the process allows the board to check the content, operational expectations, and adherence to board policy while using the monitoring to report progress. The board also has an inspection process. The inspection process, developed by John Carver, has three reports:

Values Governance

Figure 22.1. Values Governance® Model. *Source*: Copyright © 2016, Chuck Namit, Strategem LLC, Values Governance®

    a. Internal report: The CEO or designated staff member makes a report to the board.

    b. External report: The board can ask for an outside consultant or firm to do an audit or inspection of an issue or policy (this is the most used reporting process).

    c. Inspection by the board: The board will do the inspection.

3. Create a Mountain Peak of Governance by developing the Sky Bridge of Monitoring: The board creates a Mountain Peak of Governance by monitoring the organizational expectations, as well as identifying the parallel leadership of the CGO and the CEO. The role of the parallel leadership is to demonstrate the board's leadership role in policies and important decisions while figuratively sending the CEO down off the mountaintop and into the valley of detail to work through the operational expectations (means) of dealing with the organization's governance. Simply put, this is an essential way to explain the roles of the board and the CEO.

4. Develop an integrated assessment and evaluation system that includes a board self-assessment and the evaluation process. (Chapter 6 discusses the board

self-assessment and the superintendent evaluation systems.) It is equally important to assess the board and evaluate the superintendent, just as we assess the children in a school district. The board self-assessment and the superintendent evaluation identify the strengths and weaknesses of the district leadership. It is the accountability system to the owners for the school district leadership.

5. Engage the school and community to rate the schools: The organization and community score the schools in the fields of (a) trust, (b) relationship with the community, and (c) belief in the schools. The research of Karen L. Mapp rates each school as follows: (a) Fortress School (Below-Basic School), (b) Come-If-We-Call School (Basic School), (c) Open-Door School (Proficient School), and (d) Partnership School (Advanced School). Rating your schools is an excellent way to engage your community, with the schools as the focus, as a method to improve the schools.

6. Adopt a research-based curriculum and instruction program to improve student achievement: This validates the model's value that student learning is the primary goal of the organization: the public schools. Research-based curriculum is some tough educational work that involves all phases of the educational community—from the board, superintendent, administrators, principals, teachers, paraprofessionals—to engaging the parents, community, and stakeholders.

7. Create a set of Values Governance® principles to establish your new governance system: Board members need to examine the school district values to begin to design the school district governance model. Principles and values form the basis for representing your stakeholders and owners.

8. Energize the community engagement process to develop a two-way governance system: These methods demonstrate a two-way governance process, as well as an ongoing method of communication between the leaders—the board and the CEO—and the owners.

9. Develop an annual calendar of events that describes the various processes of governance. Specifically, the processes would be a leadership calendar that includes the following:

   a. Monitoring the superintendent and the organization's performance
   b. Development of a research-based curriculum
   c. Board self-assessment and the superintendent evaluation instruments (schedule the timing using the instruments)
   d. Contractual relations with the superintendent, using the assistance of outside legal counsel

Now it's time to take the information in the chapters and the chapter application-opportunity portion of the book and move from a poor or an average governance and administrative management, and turn the tables and create a new type of governance: Values Governance® system that will create dynamic school governance.

What We've Learned in the Application-Opportunity

Theme: A board must move from troublesome governance to developing a successful governance model when it uses principle values and wise governance elements.

We must move from average school district governance and behavior and turn the tables to become a successful school governance. These new changes include the following:

1. Develop a set of values principles for governance.
2. Define the roles of the board and the CEO leadership.
3. Monitor organizational expectations—throughout the year—as a method to form the basis of the superintendent evaluation.
4. Create a Mountain Peak of Governance by developing the Sky Bridge of Monitoring.
5. Assure public accountability of the district leadership by employing a board self-assessment and a superintendent evaluation.
6. Engage the school and community in rating the schools.
7. Adopt a research-based curriculum and instruction program to improve student achievement.
8. Establish a policy control status.
9. Energize community engagement to develop a two-way governance system.
10. Develop an annual governance calendar of events.

Conclusion

Throughout the book, we've seen many "bends in the road" as the school district deals with issues that provide elements of change in their district. Change requires the board members and the superintendent to use the tools, applications, and opportunities to engage with each issue and to communicate and engage the community as the owners of the district while developing their governance system.

The "turns in the road"—like *diversity*—create new challenges and issues that the school district and community must and should face as they lead the school district.

Now you've finished your essential and advanced learning by reading the twenty-two chapters of this book to start and continue your public service. As we mentioned in the beginning of the book: *have a learner's attitude!*

The old adages apply: keep listening, learning, and collaborating with other board members. Remember, it's the board that makes decisions, not the individual board members. The focus must always be on the children. As a board member, that's your job.

Finally, if you want to learn more skills, applications, and opportunities, you have many resources. In this regard, I am always willing to help board members, superintendents, public servants, executive directors, state associations, and consultants. You can contact me at: Cmapper@comcast.net.

Glossary

Alternative Governance Systems: These governance models are the Policy Governance® system (developed in 1990; 1997; *see* Principle-Based Developed List) and the Coherent Governance® system (developed in 2011). Both of these alternative governance systems differ from the traditional governance system because both systems have the following categories of policies that deal very specifically with the board's and superintendent's roles:

- *Governance Process or Governance Culture:* These are the values that the board uses to govern itself and the school district.
- *Board-CEO Relations:* This defines the roles of the board directing the organization and delegating to the CEO/superintendent using the operational performance to accomplish the goals or results of the school district.
- *Executive Limitations or Operational Expectations:* This is the ethical approach that the board expects in the governance of the school district by the use of the superintendent's means (operational expectations), monitoring reports of any reasonable actions, directions, or tasks taken to achieve the expected ends or results.
- *Ends or Results:* Achievement of school district outcomes or results for the owners, stakeholders, and community.

Benchmark Assessment: The process of incremental views of student performance data—taken periodically throughout the course of instruction. Student progress is monitored, so teachers can adjust the instructional strategies.

Board-CEO-Superintendent Relations: The delineation of the roles in which the board is the direction setter while the superintendent manages the operational performance; this allows for greater efficiency, effectiveness, and coherence in the governance structure and system.

Checking and Charting Schools: The ability for a school district—along with the community—to gauge trust, relationship, and belief in the schools. Karen L. Mapp's research lists schools in four stages: Fortress School (Below-Basic School), Come-If-We-Call School (Basic School), Open-Door School (Proficient School), and Partnership School (Advanced School).

Communication Styles: Learning your communication style allows board members and the CEO/superintendent to understand that each person has a different style that includes behavior characteristics and potential strengths and weaknesses. This promotes the board's ability to learn to work together as a team and effectively interact with the superintendent, staff, parents, and the broader community.

Community Engagement: The board engages the community, stakeholders, and business leaders by providing information regarding the achievement level of students, as well as methods the community/business leaders can use to work with schools to help shape successes and correct problems. Illustrations of high-energy community engagement projects are presented in the book and include Project 1: a school-community engagement institute and Project 2: a ten-step community engagement facilitated planning model.

Goals: The school board's plan, at a policy level, toward reaching a result for the school district that it expects to achieve. Typically, a board uses a three-tiered goal development approach that includes board-, district-, and global-level goals.

Governance: The board's role in establishing its authority—through election or appointment to office—and setting the direction for the organization.

Governance Profile Scale (GPS): A process that allows a board member to establish his or her governance preference toward policies that are task-focused, moderate, or relationship-focused.

Leadership Assessment and Evaluation: Developed techniques and instruments for an annual board self-assessment and superintendent evaluation to provide the community—owners—with assured accountability of the school district leadership.

Monitoring: A reporting process that is used by the board to check on the CEO's performance by evaluating the quality of content and adherence to board policy. The monitoring process first requires the examination of the policy and then the collection of data to determine whether the CEO is in compliance or non compliance with the policy. The board directs the superintendent-to-employee operational expectations—methods and techniques used by the CEO—to accomplish or meet the school district goals (ends or results). It is often said that if the CEO accomplishes the goals, then the school district meets the goals.

Organization: A school district—or any nonprofit or for-profit group—that is developed or created to meet and accomplish the needs of the stakeholders, community, and owners.

Policy: An ethical, prudent course of action or guiding principles developed by a school board to reach a goal or result.

Principle-Based Developed List: The development of school district principles—by the board members, with the assistance of the superintendent, cabinet, and community—forming the basis from which to create a set of policies for a locally developed governance model. This process works with all governance models discussed in this book such as the traditional, policy, coherent, and values governance models.

Research-Based Curriculum: A full range of academic courses available to students in a school district—courses that have research available to measure student progress and success while increasing student achievement.

School District Audit: A thorough examination and evaluation—with a report of the results—of the school district curriculum, showing strengths and weaknesses of each school, administration, and staff. The purpose of the audit is for the school district to move toward comprehensive school improvement.

Traditional Governance System (Developed in the Mid-1980s): The model defines the roles of the board and the superintendent. It uses the Green-Line Clock Model: everything above the 9:00 to 3:00 line—known as green line hours—is the "board's domain" while everything below is the "administrative domain." The duties and responsibilities are outlined for each of the domains. The majority of school districts around the country use the traditional model for their governance.

Values Governance® System (Developed in 2015): The school board adopts the following strategies to engage the stakeholders, community, and owners: (1) review and implement the eight important governance steps, (2) assess its existing school district policies that will improve student learning, (3) change or develop new policies to improve student learning, and (4) engage the public in ways that affect the student learning process.

Notes

Part 1

1. For the purposes of this book, the words "CEO" and "superintendent" are used interchangeably.

Chapter 1

1. Note on sources of material: The author worked for the Washington State School Directors' Association (WSSDA). He created the Passport to Leadership curriculum, satellite telecast manuals, printed curriculum, online learning curriculum, workshop manuals, and PowerPoint presentations as the training materials for the school board members, superintendents, and WSSDA consultants. Many of the ideas, approaches, models, and innovations that are used in this book were developed by the author. Moreover, following retirement from WSSDA, many ideas and approaches have been developed as a result of the author's work. WSSDA has given the author permission to use these materials.

The *District Administration Magazine* has given the author permission to use the material in the following articles: "Turning the Tables on Assessment," "Superintendent Evaluation: Here Are Keys to a Successful Superintendent Evaluation," and "Sharpening a District Leadership Model," *District Administration Magazine*, Professional Media Group LLC, vol. 44, no. 13, Norwalk, CT., November and December 2008: First of a Two-Part Series: "Turning the Tables on Assessment," and second of a two-part series: "Sharpening a District Leadership Model."

2. U.S. Census Bureau, School Districts—People and Households—U.S. Census Bureau, accessed June 15, 2012. www.census.gov.

3. David A. Steele, adapted from the "Green-Line Clock Model," National School Boards Association, 2002.

4. Chuck Namit, "Sharpening a District Leadership Model," *District Administration Magazine* (December 2008), 56; and Chuck Namit, "Demystifying School Governance," Washington State School Directors' Association (WSSDA), Olympia, WA, 11.

Chapter 2

1. John Carver and Miriam Carver, *Reinventing Your Board* (San Francisco: Jossey-Bass Publishers, 1997), 15.

2. *Board Governance Guidebook*, Missouri School Boards' Association (Columbia, Missouri: 2100 I-70 Drive Southwest, 1997), 12–13.

3. First of a Two-Part Series: "Turning the Tables on Assessment," and Second of a Two-Part Series: "Sharpening a District Leadership Model," *District Administration Magazine* in November and December 2008.

4. John Carver, *Boards That Make a Difference* (San Francisco: Jossey-Bass Publishers, 1990), 34.

5. "Sharpening a District Leadership Model," 57.

6. Carver Training in the Advanced Policy Governance Academy—October 20–24, 2003; and "Sharpening a District Leadership Model," 57.

7. Ibid.

8. Randy Quinn and Linda J. Dawson, *Good Governance Is a Choice: A Way to Re-create Your Board—the Right Way* (Lanham, Maryland: Rowman & Littlefield Education, 2011), 46–48.

9. Linda J. Dawson and Randy Quinn, *Boards That Matter* (Lanham, Maryland: Rowman & Littlefield Education, 2011), X.

Chapter 5

1. Randy Quinn and Linda J. Dawson, *Good Governance*, 71.

2. Edward deBono, Presentation on February 25–26, 1989, *Creative Learning International* in Vancouver, BC, Canada.

Chapter 6

1. Chuck Namit, "Turning the Tables on Assessment."

2. Ken O'Connor, 2007, "Classroom Assessment for Student Learning" (a Seattle workshop presentation for an Effective School for teachers and administrators), 13.

3. "Turning the Tables on Assessment," 60.

4. North Thurston Public Schools (WA), 2014–15, Board Self-Assessment Instrument.

5. North Thurston Public Schools (WA), 2014–15, Evaluation Instrument.

6. Ibid.

7. Board—Superintendent Relations, 2004, Washington State School Directors' Association (WSSDA) manual, Olympia, WA, 49.

8. *Passport to Leadership: Know Thy Self, Know Thy Board: Participant Manual*, 1998, Washington State School Directors' Association, 27.

Note: "The Board Self-Assessment and Superintendent Evaluation" (figure 6.2) process has been adapted from an approach used by the Iowa School Board Association material.

Chapter 7

1. Karen L. Mapp, "The Why, What and How of Effective School, Family and Community Partnership," Presentation at the 2007 Washington State School Directors' Association (WSSDA) Conference, and "The Why, What and How of Effective School, Family and Community Partnership," 2004 PowerPoint document (frame no.18).

2. Ibid., 7.

3. Karen L. Mapp, 2012. *Moving Forward: Building the Capacity for Effective Family Engagement* (Notes on citations: Fortress School, 11; Come-If-We-Call School, 12; Open-Door School, 13; and Partnership School, 14), 11–13.

4. An adaptation of the concept and description of the stages presented in D. Mabry and D. Bevars, *Cases in Labor Relations and Collective Bargaining* (New York: The Ronald Press Co., 1966).

5. Sources: The model is adapted from the following sources: (A) Presentation by Karen L. Mapp, at the 2007 Washington State School Directors' Association (WSSDA) Conference; (B) an adaptation of a leadership model presented in Kenneth H. Blanchard and Paul Hersey, *Management of Organizational Behavior: Utilizing Human Resources*, 4th Ed. (Englewood Cliffs, NJ: Prentice Hall, Inc., 1981); and (C) an adaptation of the concept and description of the stages presented in Mabry and Bevars, *Cases in Labor Relations and Collective Bargaining* (New York: The Ronald Press Co., 1966).

Source note: The concept of low, moderate, and high levels of trust, relationship, and belief to describe each of the four stages was adapted from a leadership model presented in Blanchard and Hersey, *Management of Organizational Behavior*.

6. Mapp, *Moving Forward*, 11.

7. Ibid., 12.

8. Ibid., 13.

9. Ibid., 14.

Chapter 8

1. Randy Quinn, and Linda J. Dawson, *Good Governance*, 44.

2. A memo to the North Thurston Public Schools Board, February 3, 2005, "Board Approval of Effective Schools Consulting Services."

3. "Learning 24/7 Consulting Firm Report," North Thurston Public Schools Audit October 2004.

4. The material on the North Thurston Public Schools' implementation of Effective Schools was produced by Joe Belmonte, former Assistant Superintendent, Elementary Education. Joe Belmonte was instrumental in the development of the Effective Schools.

5. The *Olympian* editorial on the "24/7 Consulting Firm Audit of the North Thurston Public Schools' Audit of the School System," December 4, 2004.

6. Ibid.

7. 2015–16 North Thurston Strategic Plan: Committed to Excellence in Student Learning. September 18, 2015, 2–6.

Chapter 9

1. The communication instrument is an adaption that simulates the Myer-Briggs instrument, which will give readers an impression of their communication style.
(Note: The reader can purchase a short version of the actual Myer-Briggs instrument: see Consulting Psychologists Press, Inc.) Also see the 2009 book by Robert Bolton and Dorothy Grover Bolton, *People Styles at Work . . . and Beyond: Making Bad Relationships Good and Good Relationships Better*, and take the communication instrument.

2. The terms "intuition," "feeler," "sensor," and "thinker" have been adapted from the following sources: "Find out How Your Journal Personality May Be at Odds." *Working Smart,* The Executive Service from Learning International, vol. 3, no. 1, January 1986, and "What's My Communication Style?" presented in a Washington State Government Entry Management Core Program.

3. The Governance Profile Scale (GPS) is an adaption of material from the Washington State School Directors' (WSSDA) work. The WSSDA model was adapted from the Personnel Management Program Services instrument, Michigan State University (MSU), 1970. (Note: Verbal permission was granted to the WSSDA to adapt the material; however, WSSDA does not have a letter of permission.) The MSU model appeared to be an adaptation from Robert Blake and Jane Mouton, New Managerial Grid (Gulf Publishing Co., 1978), 119.

4. Ibid.

5. Certain aspects of the GPS model are adapted from Fred Fiedler's research material (e.g., task-focused, moderate, or relationship-focused approach) to gauge board member behavior. (Note: Fred Fiedler's books include Contingency Model Matching Leadership Style to a Situation, which is featured in the following publications: F. E. Fiedler and M. Chemers, 1974. "Leadership and Effective Management," Reprinted in Hampton, et al., 624–5, and F. E. Fiedler and M. Chemers, Improving Leadership Effectiveness: The Leader Match Concept, 2nd ed. (New York: John Wiley & Sons, 1984).

6. The concept of Any Reasonable Interpretation (ARI) was developed by John Carver for his Policy Governance® model, John Carver and Miriam Mayhew

Carver, *Reinventing Your Board* (San Francisco: Jossey-Bass Inc., 1997) 22, 24–25, 59, 62, 73, 87, 92, 129.

Chapter 10

1. Linda J. Dawson and Randy Quinn, *Boards That Matter*, 82.
2. Ibid., 81.
3. Chuck Namit and Bob Hughes, "Energizing the Engagement of the Community in Governance: The School Board's Role in Governance Is Vital to be Successful in Leading the School District," *District Administration Magazine,* February 2014, Professional Opinion, 1–3.
4. Ibid., 7.
5. Bob Hughes—as a Boeing executive—developed the concept of businesses assisting schools with grants to state school board associations; he was also a former member of the Washington State Board of Education, 2015.
6. "Energizing the Engagement of the Community in Governance," 7–8.
7. Ibid., 8–9. Chuck Namit is a school board member, North Thurston Public Schools, and developed the concept of two-way governance, 2015.
8. Note: *District Administration Magazine* has given the author permission to use the material in this chapter that was taken from the article "Energizing the engagement of the community in governance."

Chapter 12

1. Chuck Namit, "Demystifying School Governance," Washington State School Directors' Association publication, 2006, 11.
2. Ibid., 16.
3. Ibid., 16–17.

Chapter 13

1. John Carver and Miriam Carver, *Reinventing Your Board*, 15.
Note: Also: How Does the TAASA Board Do Business? (n.d.). Retrieved from http://www.ncdsv.org/images/TAASA_How-does-the-Board-Do-Business, 2013.pdf; the site quotes John Carver. (Note: I have directly quoted John Carver.)
2. John Carver, *Boards That Make a Difference*, 34.
3. Source of Information: The concepts of "service trademark, ownership of the model, and the purity of the model" were emphasized by John Carver to consultants throughout the training at the John Carver's Policy Governance® Academy, October 22–24, 2003, in Atlanta, GA.
4. Linda J. Dawson and Randy Quinn, *Boards That Matter*, 4.

Note: Also: "What Is Policy Governance," December 1, 2016. Retrieved from http://www.leading-resources.com/wp-content/uploads/2015/08/What-Is-Policy-Gover.

Chapter 15

1. Edward deBono, *Six Thinking Hats* (New York: Viking Penguin, 1985), 135.
2. Reproduced from a *District Administration* sidebar article, "Dallas' Failures Can Be Remedied: Sharpening a District's Leadership Model," December 2008.

Chapter 16

1. Chuck Namit, "Turning the Tables on Assessment," 58.
2. Ibid., 58–59.
3. Ken O'Connor, "Classroom Assessment," 13.
4. Chuck Namit, "Sharpening a District Leadership Model," 58–59.
5. Note: Source of material: Superintendent Evaluation Tool Box, October 2016. Retrieved from https://www.districtadministration.com/article/superintendent-evaluation-tool-box.
6. North Thurston Public Schools (WA), 2014–2015, Superintendent Evaluation Instrument.
7. North Thurston Public Schools (WA), 2014–2015, Board Self-Assessment Instrument.
8. Chuck Namit, "Turning the Tables on Assessment," 60.
9. Chuck Namit, "Sharpening a District Leadership Model," 58.

Chapter 17

1. Karen L. Mapp, presented at 2007 WSSDA Conference; Karen L. Mapp, *Moving Forward: Building the Capacity for Effective Family Engagement*, 2012 (Notes: Fortress School, 11; Come If-We-Call School, 12; Open-Door School, 13; and Partnership School, 14).
2. Ibid., 11–14.
3. Learning 24/7 Consultant firm audit of the North Thurston Public Schools, Effective Schools Assessment, October 2004, 3–6.
4. Karen L. Mapp, *Moving Forward*, 11–14.

Chapter 18

1. Randy Quinn and Linda J. Dawson, *Good Governance*, 44.
2. 24/7 Learning Consultant Firm, North Thurston Public Schools Audit, Dr. Hal Guthrie, Dr. Ray Garcia, and Robert Skaife, October 2004.

3. Source of the information: The material on the North Thurston Public Schools implementation of the Effective Schools was produced by Joe Belmonte, former assistant superintendent, elementary education. (Joe Belmonte was instrumental in the development of the Effective Schools), http://www.nthurston.k12.wa.us/site/default.aspx?PageID=1.

4. Ibid.

5. North Thurston Public Schools Strategic Plan: Committed to Excellence in Student Learning, September 18, 2015, 2–6. Retrieved from http://www.nthurstonK12wa.us/cms/lib/W15%20.

6. 2015–16 North Thurston School District Goals, February 20, 2015, 1–7. Retrieved from http://www.nthurston.k12.wa.us/cms/lib/WA01001371/Centricity/Domain/6/, 2014–15.

7. 2014–15 Superintendent's Mid-Year Performance Discussion, January 28, 2015.

8. Ibid.

9. Ibid.

10. Ibid.

11. Ibid.

12. Ibid.

13. Ibid.

14. Ibid.

15. Ibid.

16. Ibid.

17. 2015–16 NTPS Goal Development and Progress Report, December 7, 2015.

Chapter 19

1. Adapted from the following source: "Find out How Your Job and Personality May Be at Odds," Working Smart, The Executive Advisory Service from Learning International, vol. 3, no. 1, January 1986.

2. Adapted from an exercise developed by Chuck Namit in the publication Know Thy Self, Know Thy Board, 1998. Washington State School Directors' Association (WSSDA). Adapted from Entry Management Development Core Program, State of Washington; Effective Communication, Level 1, Washington State. (AO G:02) 25.

Chapter 20

1. Source of Information: The Governance Profile Scale (GPS) is an adaptation of material from the Personnel Management Program Services instrument, Michigan State University (MSU), 1970. Permission was granted to the Washington State School Directors' Association (WSSDA). (Note 1: The MSU model appears to be an adaptation from Robert Blake and Jane Mouton, *The New Managerial Grid* (Gulf Publishing Co., 1978), 11. Additionally, the development of the Governance Profile Scale (GPS) also used other research in its adaptation: Fred Fiedler's research

material (task-focused, moderate, or relationship-focused approach) is utilized to gauge board member behavior. (Note 2: Fred Fiedler's books include *Contingency Model Matching Leadership Style to a Situation.* The following publications feature Fiedler's research: F. E. Fiedler and M. M. Chemers, "Leadership and Effective Management," reprinted in Hampton, et al., 1974, 624–25; and F. E. Fiedler and M. M. Chemers, *Improving Leadership Effectiveness: The Leader Match Concept*, 2nd ed. (New York: John Wiley & Sons, 1984), 11.)

2. Ibid.

Note 1: The Governance Grid scale is adapted from the following sources: (1) H. Mescon, Michael Albert and Franklin Khedouri, *Management* (New York: Harper & Row, 1985), 495–97; (2) Ibid., 537; (3) Ibid., 535–37.

Note 2: The Governance Grid is adapted from the following resources: (1) Robert Blake and Jane Mouton, *New Managerial Grid*, and (2) a Personnel Management Program Services Instrument, Michigan State University, that adapted a model based on the Blake and Mouton model.

Chapter 21

1. Thom Hartmann, *Cracking the Code: How to Win Hearts, Change Minds, and Restore America's Original Vision* (San Francisco: Berrett-Koehler Publishers, 2007), 2.

2. Ibid., 5.

3. Ibid., 5–6.

4. Ibid., 7.

5. Ibid., 3.

6. Chuck Namit and Bob Hughes, "Energizing the Engagement of the Community in Governance," *District Administration*, February 2014, Professional Opinion, 6.

7. http://www.districtadministration.com/article/energizing-engagement-community-governance.

8. Ibid., 6–9.

9. Adapted from *Engaging Parents and Community as Stakeholders in Our Schools: An Institute for School Boards and Their District Teams.* The Institute was produced by WSSDA in partnership with the Northwest Regional Educational Laboratory, Washington Alliance for Better Schools, Washington Education Association, and underwritten by a grant from Washington Mutual Bank, 179–82.

10. Adapted from a presentation, "Community Engagement: Involving Parents and the Community in Our Schools," developed by Chuck Namit for the WSSDA and presented at the 2007 NSBA Conference, 182–87.

11. *Community Engagement and Stakeholder Linkages, Module 1*, June 29, 2005. Washington State School Directors' Association (WSSDA) Online Course at Seattle Pacific University.

12. Adapted from a presentation by David Langford, *Teams* (Billings, MT: Langford International, Inc., 1995).

Note on the source of the material for this chapter: The District Administration magazine has given the author permission to use the material in this chapter that was taken from the following article: Chuck Namit and Bob Hughes, "Energizing the Engagement of the Community in Governance: The School Board's Role in Governance Is Vital to be Successful in Leading the School District," District Administration, Professional Media Group LLC, February 2014, Professional Opinion.

About the Author

 **Chuck Namit** is an education and nonprofit consultant and is president of Strategem, LLC, governance and leadership group that provides training, facilitation, board self-assessment, CEO and superintendent evaluation, CEO coaching, and governance training services for the public schools and the community. The firm provides governance training in Values Governance®, board governance, CEO coaching, development training, and conference presentations.

Namit developed and managed a fourteen-member cadre of board development and governance trainers as assistant executive director for the Washington State School Directors' Association (WSSDA) for fifteen years. He trains school board members, CEOs, and administrators as a consultant for the WSSDA. He developed a multilevel, integrated school board curriculum for first term through experienced board members.

Namit was trained by John Carver in Policy Governance® at his Advanced Academy. He has worked with Boeing executives to develop a model for implementing continuous improvement through strategic planning in schools. The work of the Boeing Corporation and Namit on this program earned the Conference Board Award. He has been involved in the exploration of change in education reform and has developed community-wide change programs. Namit also has served as a member of the National School Board Foundation task force on Data-Driven Decision Making. He has trained municipal employees in supervision and management. He has taught at the community college level and served as an adjunct professor at Seattle Pacific University, and has developed online training for school board members and superintendents.

Namit presents regularly at the National School Board Association (NSBA) annual conferences and has trained board members and administrators for more than thirty years. He was on the faculty of the National School Board Association Boot Camp for new board members. Namit received the NSBA's 2006 Shannon Award for excellence and innovation in school board training.

Namit attended Portland Public Schools, Oregon, and graduated from Central Catholic High School. He went on to earn a BS degree in history, with a minor in political science, from Portland State University. Namit also earned an MEd degree from Oregon State University (involved in the National Teacher Corps program), a master's degree in communication (journalism) from Michigan State University (thesis: "UAW and GM Attitudes toward the 1970 Strike"), and an MBA degree from the University of Puget Sound (management, marketing, and human development).

Namit is in his sixth term as a member of the North Thurston Public Schools Board of Directors, a board member of the WSSDA, and council member on the Thurston Regional Planning Council.

CPSIA information can be obtained
at www.ICGtesting.com
Printed in the USA
BVOW09s0227261017

498586BV00001B/1/P